T0268693

**Other titles published as part of the 1992 Ubu Repertory
Theater Festival of New Works include:**

Nowhere by Reine Bartève (Published with *A Man with Women*)
The Best of Schools by Jean-Marie Besset
The White Bear by Daniel Besnehard
Family Portrait by Denise Bonal

**Other individual play titles available from
Ubu Repertory Theater Publications are:**

Swimming Pools at War by Yves Navarre

Night Just Before The Forest and *Struggle of the Dogs and the Black* by
Bernard-Marie Koltès

The Fetishist by Michel Tournier

The Office by Jean-Paul Aron

Far From Hagondange and *Vater Land, the Country of our Fathers* by
Jean-Paul Wenzel

Deck Chairs by Madeleine Laïk

The Passport and *The Door* by Pierre Bourgeade

The Showman by Andrée Chedid

Madame Knipper's Journey to Eastern Prussia by Jean-Luc Lagarce

Passengers by Daniel Besnehard

Cabale by Enzo Corman

Enough is Enough by Protais Asseng

A Tempest by Aimé Césaire

Monsieur Thôgô-gnigni by Bernard Dadié

The Glorious Destiny of Marshal Nnikon Nniku by Tchicaya u Tam'Si

Parentheses of Blood by Sony Labou Tansi

Intelligence Powder by Kateb Yacine

The Sea Between Us by Denise Chalem

Country Landscapes by Jacques-Pierre Amette

Anthologies available from
Ubu Repertory Theater Publications:

Afrique I: New Plays from the Congo, Ivory Coast, Senegal and Zaire, including *The Daughter of the Gods* by Abdou Anta Kâ, *Equatorium* by Maxime N'Debeka, *Lost Voices* by Diur N'Tumb, *The Second Ark* by Sony Lab'ou Tansi, and *The Eye* by Bernard Zadi Zaourou. Preface by George C. Wolfe.

Afrique II: New Plays from Madagascar, Mauritania and Togo including *The Legend of Wagadu as Seen by Sia Yatabere* by Moussa Diagana, *The Crossroads* by Josué Kossi Efoui, *The Herd* by Charlotte-Arrisoa Rafenomanjato, *The Prophet and the President* by Jean-Luc Raharimanana and *The Singing Tortoise* and *Yevi's Adventures in Monsterland* by Sénouvo Agbota Zinsou. Preface by Henry Louis Gates, Jr.

Gay Plays: An International Anthology, including *The Function* by Jean-Marie Besset, *A Tower Near Paris* and *Grand Finale* by Copi, *Return of the Young Hippolytus* by Hervé Dupuis, *Ancient Boys* by Jean-Claude van Itallie, and *The Lives and Deaths of Miss Shakespeare* by Liliane Wouters. Preface by Catherine Temerson and Françoise Kourilsky.

Plays by Women: An International Anthology including *A Picture Perfect Sky* by Denise Bonal, *Jocasta* by Michèle Fabien, *The Girls from the Five and Ten* by Abla Farhoud, *You Have Come Back* by Fatima Gallaire-Bourega, and *Your Handsome Captain* by Simone Schwarz-Bart. Preface by Catherine Temerson and Françoise Kourilsky.

The Paris Stage: Recent Plays including *A Birthday Present for Stalin* by Jean Bouchard, *The Rest Have Got It Wrong* by Jean-Michel Ribes, *The Sleepless City* by Jean Tardieu, *Trumpets of Death* by Tilly, and *The Neighbors* by Michel Vinaver. Preface by Catherine Temerson and Françoise Kourilsky.

Theater and Politics: An International Anthology including *Black Wedding Candles for Blessed Antigone* by Sylvain Bemba, *A Season in the Congo* by Aimé Césaire, *Burn River Burn* by Jean-Pol Fargeau, *Olympe and the Executioner* by Wendy Kesselman and *Mephisto*, adapted from Klaus Mann by Ariane Mnouchkine. Preface by Erika Munk.

Jean-Louis Bourdon

Jock

translated from the French by

Timothy Johns

Printed in the United States of America

ISBN: 0-913745-3-75

Jock had its American premiere at Ubu
Repertory Theater, 15 West 28th Street, New
York, NY 10001 on May 5, 1992.

Director:	**André Ernotte**
Set Designer:	**John Brown**
Lighting Designer:	**Greg MacPherson**
Costume Designer:	**Carol Ann Pelletier**
Sound Designers:	**Phil Lee and**
	David Lawson

Cast, in order of appearance:

Craig Wasson	JOCK
Jim Abele	JIMMY
Margaret Klenck	SONIA

Produced by **Ubu Repertory Theater**
Françoise Kourilsky, *Artistic Director*

Characters, in order of appearance:

JOCK

JIMMY

SONIA

(A rather untidy interior, dark and musty. There's a table in the middle of the room. In one corner is a double bed with a curtain on one side. Front right is a wooden service bar.

There are three doors: the front door is at the left rear; the door to the cellar at right rear; the door to the kitchen on the other side of the bar, to the left. Toward the left rear is a window. There's also a creaky rocking chair, and a few other chairs besides. On the wall hangs a shotgun.

JOCK is lying in bed. On a chair by his side, a radio is playing jazz.

After a moment, JIMMY enters.

JOCK lowers the volume.)

JOCK *(not looking at JIMMY)*: Where you been?

JIMMY *(taking off his coat, with a tired look)*: I've been out.

JOCK: I can see you've been out. You get the papers? *(JIMMY doesn't answer.)* I said: Did you get the newspapers?

JIMMY: No.

JOCK *(with a look of outrage)*: What!? You didn't buy the papers?

JIMMY *(indifferent)*: That's right.

JOCK *(slight pause)*: Not one little rag?

1

JIMMY: Nope. Not a one.

JOCK: And yet you know your big brother likes to read the news when he wakes up. Don't you know that? You know he loves to read the morning news over his coffee! Fix me some coffee.

(JIMMY *goes into the kitchen; after a moment he returns.*)

Get to know the facts with the rise of the sun, that's what I like; understand what kind of world I'm waking up in. You know?

JIMMY: Let me tell you, Jock, you're coming into a world where the sun's been up for ages already. . . even if we don't see much of it anymore.

JOCK: Ya wanna know something, Jimmy? Sometimes you make me want to shit!

(JIMMY *goes to the kitchen and comes back with* JOCK's *coffee.*)

Hey, Jimmy, what's the world like for today?

JIMMY *(detached, he sits down at the table and starts drawing)*: What I suppose you really mean is, what day is it today.

JOCK: You know goddamn well what I mean, so don't play dumb. I'm asking you where I can safely set foot. Today! *(after a moment)* Anything blow up last night?

JIMMY *(still detached)*: As usual.

JOCK *(not very convinced)*: Oh? Nothing more than usual?

JIMMY: No.

JOCK *(after a while)*: There's one more thing I would really like to know. *(slight pause)* I said, there's one more thing I'd like to know!

JIMMY *(still the same)*: What's that?

JOCK *(slight pause)*: What did I do last night? Did I go to the game?

JIMMY *(still detached)*: No, you slept.

JOCK *(with a strange look)*: Don't bullshit me, Jimmy, you know I can't sleep through a game! You wanna know the truth, it's your own damn memory lapses you're foistin' off on me, that's the truth of the matter, and now I don't even remember how we Mastodons did last night.

JIMMY: You didn't play.

(JOCK bursts out laughing.)

JOCK: Didn't play! Us? *(He laughs again.)* What are you tryin' to say? There's not a single team in the playoffs can hold a candle to us, and you know it! The Mastodons can chew up and spit out any other team there is, okay, Jimmy?! So just stick that up your pipe, okay? *(slight pause)* There's just one thing I'd like to know, and that's how much the other team got crushed, that's all I'd like to know. By how much.

JIMMY: Nobody got crushed.

JOCK *(annoyed)*: I'm warning you, kid, you're asking for it!

JIMMY *(impassive)*: Jock. You don't play anymore. Anyway, the playoffs have been over for months.

JOCK *(bursts out laughing)*: I see the game with my own eyes and the guy tells me the playoffs are over! *(Laughs some more.)* Jimmy, you scare me. I'm starting to wonder if I'm gonna be able to do anything for you. This has me worried.

JIMMY *(still impassive, still drawing; after a while)*: We went over to Kate's last night.

JOCK *(looks surprised)*: Kate, my fiancée?

JOCK: She's not your fiancée anymore.

(JOCK glares at JIMMY as if insulted.)

JOCK: Whattaya, tryin' to pick a fight, Jimmy? Jesus! I swear the kid is jealous. *(He laughs like he can't get over it.)* Kate—not my fiancée anymore! *(Laughs again.)* I told you you shoulda seen a doctor, kid. These lapses are no joke! One of these days you're gonna crack up right before my very eyes. *(He looks sad for his brother, then begins to laugh again.)* And since when is she not supposed to be my fiancée.

JIMMY *(the same)*: Since she got married.

JOCK *(dumbfounded)*: Kate! Married?! *(with a worried look)* Jimmy?

4

(JIMMY *glances at him and returns to his drawing.)*

Jimmy, are you all right?

JIMMY *(turns to* JOCK*)*: Just fine, Jock, thanks.

JOCK *(still astonished; a slight pause)*: And. . . Who's she supposed to be married to? (JIMMY *doesn't reply.)* I'm talking to you! Who to?

JIMMY *(ever the same)*: To Norman. (JOCK's *eyes get big and round.)* That'll be fourteen years come April.

JOCK *(stupefied)*: Fourteen years. . . this April. *(looks disappointed; after a slight pause)* The goddamn little bitch! *(He finishes his coffee, with a thoughtful air.)* And with Norman on top of it all! Kate and Norman? Just who do you think's gonna believe that? Whattya tryin' to say? That I don't read the papers every day, and in particular Marriages and Obituaries? Huh? And by the way, run get me the papers, will ya? I need to keep in touch with current affairs, ya know? This is absolutely essential for me. Each and every person should feel concerned with the movement of his planet. *(slight pause)* I'd like to know if it's turning in the right direction—we all have our role to play, right, kiddo? And the simple act of getting acquainted with the news of the day is an obligation to all humanity. Ya wanna know the truth, it's makin' love with your own planet. You hear me, Jimmy?

JIMMY *(ever the same)*: Yeah, I'm listening.

JOCK: Good. 'cause I'm not finished. *(He looks in his cup.)* Gimme my apple, will you? *(JIMMY gets up, goes to the kitchen, and brings back an apple for JOCK. He starts to bite into it, stops and starts polishing it. After a while.)* You want my opinion?

JIMMY *(same)*: Mmm.

JOCK *(looking at the apple)*: We don't take good enough care of it, and it doesn't give us back shit anymore. *(He takes out his knife and lifts out what looks like a little worm dangling from the end of it.)* There's Norman for you, kiddo: he's ruined my apple. *(He tosses aside the worm and bites into the apple. He chews, then suddenly:)* Hey, Jimmy! How much longer you think you're gonna dump these radioactive apples on me? With little Normans inside? *(Slight pause; he lies back down.)* Jimmy? One last time: will you please go get me the paper?

JIMMY *(somewhat annoyed)*: There are no more papers, Jock. You understand? Nothing! The stands are closed, okay? Nothing's open anymore—nothing! Go to sleep—it's better for you.

JOCK *(raising himself in bed)*: Go to sleep? You crazy? *(He gives him a strange look.)* Sometimes I wonder if while they were at it they didn't just go ahead and lobotomize you.

JIMMY *(slight pause; still drawing)*: While they were at what?

JOCK: I'm talking about your last operation!

JIMMY: You mean my appendectomy?

JOCK: Ah! now you get it.

JIMMY *(still unrattled)*: Jock—the man who operated on me was a doctor, not a butcher.

JOCK: Oh ho! Very funny, kid, very funny! Good thing I'm penned in here, I'd've rolled out of bed and broke my neck from laughter.

JIMMY: That's not what I meant.

JOCK: Oh? And just what did you mean?

JIMMY: I. . . try to get some sleep, will you? You could use a little.

JOCK: Oh yeah? Here we go again. . . and what about you, kid? Big Shot here wants me to get some sleep and I don't know what's goin' on outside my window. *(He seems to be looking for something at the foot of his bed.)* Never mind, I'll go get the paper myself. After all, why should I need you to go get the news, huh, Jimmy? *(He keeps looking.)* Where'd you put it?

JIMMY *(who's just about had it)*: Where's what?

JOCK: My leg, that's what! *(JIMMY sighs and gets up; he looks for JOCK's artificial leg under the bed, finds it, and gives it to him.)* Where was it?

JIMMY: There!

JOCK: There, where?

JIMMY *(returning to his drawing)*: Oh fuck it.

JOCK *(attaches his leg with his back to the audience)*: Some day, kid, you never know what's comin' down, but I'll tell you one goddamn thing an' you better stick this in your pipe. I don't need you. *(Pause. JOCK finishes dressing, gets up, walks over to JIMMY—with stiff leg—looks down at the drawing over his shoulder.)* What is it? *(no answer)* What're you drawing? Let's see—Ah! the great cathedral? *(bending down closer)* Looks more like a combine down the middle of Main Street! *(snickering)* Didn't anyone ever tell you it's illegal to drive a combine down Main Street? Not very realistic. *(finishes dressing)* On the other hand, you got quite a talent for farm machinery, Jimbo. Really. *(putting on his overcoat)* Some guys are good at landscapes, forests, oceans, what not, wheat fields, even. But you, it's farm machinery. Hey, you could start some kinda of a club here—The Society of Jerk-Off Faggots! *(He laughs and goes out. JIMMY keeps drawing. Blackout.)*

(Same set. JIMMY is still drawing. There's a knock at the door; JIMMY hesitates, then gets up to open. A woman stands in the doorway. They stare at each other intently.)

WOMAN *(holding a shoulder bag, softly)*: Hello, Jimmy.

JIMMY *(awkward, but obviously pleasantly surprised)*: What are. . . what are you doing here?

WOMAN: I was in the neighborhood, and just thought to myself. . .

JIMMY: Well I'm glad you did, glad you did, Sonia. Come on in.

(She enters, he closes the door without taking his eyes off her. SONIA looks around the room. He is visibly embarrassed.)

Well! It's not cleaned up but. . .

SONIA: Don't worry about it. I just wanted to see you.

JIMMY *(embarrassed)*: I uh. . . I'm glad you came. . . Can I get you a drink?

SONIA *(slow to answer)*: Sure. Why not?

JIMMY *(clearly happy, self-conscious)*: Scotch?

SONIA: Fine, sure. Scotch it'll be.

(He pours her a scotch. Meanwhile she looks at JIMMY's drawing on the table.)

I see you're still drawing. *(She picks it up.)*

JIMMY (*smiling*): Yeah, well, it passes the time.

SONIA (*peering closer at the drawing*): One thing I do know, you could go places with this.

JIMMY (*still smiling*): That's not what everyone thinks.

SONIA: So maybe some people don't know what they're talking about.

(JIMMY *hands her a drink; she puts down the drawing.*)

Thanks.

(*They look at each other intently.*)

JIMMY (*embarrassed*): Jock's out to get the paper.

SONIA: Oh! doesn't surprise me. How is he?

JIMMY: Oh, okay, pretty much the same. I think I'll have something too. (*He goes over to the bar and fixes a drink. A little troubled.*) I, uh. . . I was beginning to get worried, you know.

SONIA: Oh? About what?

JIMMY: Well. . . 'cause I hadn't had any news! (*She looks at him and smiles gently.*) If I'd only known you were coming this morning, I'd've. . .

SONIA (*interrupting*): I told you: it doesn't bother me in the slightest.

JIMMY (*seems happy; looks at her with emotion*): So. Here's to. . .

SONIA: Right. To us.

JIMMY *(noticing her packages)*: Here, let me take those.

SONIA: Oh, don't worry, it's not heavy, I brought these for you, just a few little things for the fridge.

JIMMY: I'll go put them away now.

(He goes to the kitchen. SONIA sips her drink and coughs; JIMMY comes back in.)

SONIA: I don't know where you got this, but. . .

JIMMY: It's from the new distillery. You want some water with it?

SONIA: No, no. It's fine.

(They drink.)

Where is it?

JIMMY *(thinking)*: Hmm?

SONIA: The distillery.

JIMMY: Oh! about thirty miles from here. Some guy came by the other day and what does Jock do? Buys a half dozen cases from him.

SONIA: Sounds like Jock, all right.

JIMMY: Yeah. *(They look at one another tenderly. Slight pause.)* I'm so glad you're here, sweetheart, I. . .

SONIA (*putting her finger over his mouth*): Shh! I've been wanting to see you too.

(*They stare at each other for a few more seconds.*)

JIMMY (*troubled, softly*): It's been quite a while now, huh? How long?

SONIA (*looking at him, she hesitates*): I haven't kept track.

(*She drinks. They look at each other a moment.*)

What would you say if I told you that. . . I meant to come back.

JIMMY (*not believing his ears*): You mean. . . come back. . . here?

SONIA: Yes, here. Unless that's a problem.

JIMMY (*smiling ecstatically*): What? A problem?! Are you kidding? You know, darling, you've just given me the best news I've had all year. And you wonder if it's a problem? Sonia! (*They kiss. After a moment.*) I'm glad, too, for Jock.

SONIA: I'm not coming back for him, Jimmy.

JIMMY: I know, darling, I know. (*pause*) I know you've never been crazy about Jock, but. . .

SONIA: It's you, Jim, I'm crazy about. . . Him, I've simply put up with 'cause he's your brother.

JIMMY (*very slightly annoyed*): Sonia!

SONIA: I'm sorry Jimmy, but there are some things in life, certain ways of being treated, that just don't go away.

JIMMY: Don't hold it against him, Sonia, I think he's going through some changes.

SONIA: I've been changing, too, Jim.

(He takes a drink and stares at her with a tender smile.)

JIMMY: It's funny. These last few days he hasn't stopped asking me about you. Last week, he must've asked about you a dozen times. "Hey, Jimmy, where's Sonia? You think we'll ever see her again?" And so on, stuff like that. You'd think the guy had some kind of premonition.

SONIA: Yeah, so you'd think. *(Looks at her empty glass.)*

JIMMY: Would you like another?

SONIA: Please, thanks.

(He goes to get it.)

JIMMY: I think it's gonna give him one helluva surprise, to see you here.

SONIA: How do you think he'll take it?

JIMMY *(handing her a drink)*: Very well. I'm sure he'll want to drink to this.

(They drink. JOCK enters. He looks at them, then casts a glance around the room.)

JOCK *(as if alone with his brother)*: Couldn't find one single newspaper. Probably some goddamn strike.

(He hangs up his coat and sits down in his rocker.)

JIMMY *(a little nervous)*: Jock?

JOCK *(rocking)*: Mmm? What is it now?

JIMMY *(embarrassed; after a pause)*: Don't you. . . didn't you see who's here?

JOCK *(looking around; slight pause)*: No. Who's here?

JIMMY *(hesitating)*: You don't recognize her?

JOCK *(looking at SONIA)*: No. Who is she?

JIMMY: Come on, Jock, it's Sonia! *(Pause)* She's come back to us.

JOCK *(mechanically)*: Really? How nice, how very nice. I'm very pleased to hear it. Really.

(JIMMY glances at SONIA, obviously relieved that JOCK poses no objection.)

Couldn't find one single paper, the sky's turning dark and it's hardly noon: it's beyond comprehension. You can't find a thing out there. It all seems completely deserted, practically dead—not to mention the cold, which I can't stand, by the way. And on top of it all it stinks in here. Open a window.

(After hesitating, JIMMY goes to open a window. Brief silence.)

Jimmy!?

JIMMY: Yes?

JOCK: Who is Sonia?

JIMMY: Huh? I mean. . . what's that you say?

(SONIA remains impassive and drinks in silence.)

JOCK: I said it's about time you went to see a good ear doctor, kid! I'm telling you, you're getting stone deaf, and it hurts me to have to say it. *(Much louder, but without hostility.)* I'm asking you who is this Sonia? Don't know the woman. . . *(lower)* and I think under the circumstances the best thing to do would be to introduce us. Don't you think, Miss? The best thing to do under the circumstances would be to introduce us? Jimmy, when two people are unacquainted, the best thing to do is to introduce them to each other. Miss, I want to apologize for Jimmy, he's just not got the hang of the social graces. *(Gets up and goes over to SONIA.)* Name's Jock. *(Holds out his hand.)* And you?

SONIA *(after a slight hesitation)*: Sonia.

JOCK *(shaking her hand)*: My pleasure. I'm . . . I'm absolutely delighted to meet you and to welcome you to our humble abode. What do you say, Jimmy, this calls for a drink! Bring us a round.

SONIA *(showing her glass)*: Thanks, I have plenty.

JOCK: Oh come on don't be so stupid, I said this calls for a drink! Am I right, Jimmy? This kind of event always calls for a drink. It's not every day a girl of your class pays us the courtesy of a little visit. It's been a long time since there's been a feminine presence in this house, ain't that right, kid? A long, long time.

JIMMY: That's right.

JOCK: Matter of fact the last brief visit we had goes back about two months, that was Miss Berthier it was. You know Miss Berthier?

SONIA: No, I don't believe I've had the pleasure.

JOCK *(leaning over in confidence)*: A horrible fat pig, absolutely devoid of any interest, a cheap little slut with greasy hair—and I mean greasy! So greasy poor dumb animals fall right into the trap! If you get what I mean.

SONIA: Hmm. . . yes.

JOCK: So! you can just imagine the enthusiasm I feel sharing a glass with you.

SONIA *(playing along)*: Well of course.

JOCK *(smiling)*: Thank you. Give us a double, Jimmy, my boy.

(JOCK *stares at* SONIA, *who seems a bit uncomfortable. Meanwhile* JIMMY *serves the drinks.)*

She's a knock-out, don't you think?

JIMMY *(embarrassed, he brings the drinks and hands one to* JOCK*)*: Well, yes.

JOCK *(to* SONIA *with a smile)*: So! Aside from popping in on people uninvited, what else do you do? *(*JIMMY *serves* SONIA*.)*

SONIA: Nothing.

JOCK: Jimmy!

JIMMY *(getting a little weary)*: What!?

JOCK: You know what? Sometimes I just can't understand you.

JIMMY *(amused)*: Oh?

JOCK: How many times do I have to tell you: ladies first! It's just not done, Jimmy. Sometimes I wonder who raised you. *(*JIMMY *is drinking calmly as if he didn't hear a word.)*

JOCK: *(to* SONIA*)*: So, that's your story, huh? You don't do anything.

SONIA: No.

JOCK: No. . . meaning what?

SONIA: Meaning in general, no, I don't do anything.

JOCK: Ah! . . *(smiles)* Which would seem to imply that from time to time you do do some things. . . in particular. *(laughs)*

SONIA: If you wish. It all depends on the situation. On the relationship.

JOCK *(somewhat mockingly)*: Well, now, isn't that just the truth! That is, isn't it? So! what sorta things do you sometimes find yourself doing?

SONIA *(apparently reflecting)*: Oh. . . for example. . . visiting my husband.

JOCK *(with a surprised look)*: Ah, now that's interesting! That's really very touching, at least to me. But tell me, may I ask? who is he?

SONIA: Sorry?

JOCK: Your husband. Who is he?

JIMMY *(embarrassed)*: Stop it, Jock.

JOCK *(to JIMMY)*: Hey. Jimmy. I'm not talking to you, hear? I'm talking to our visitor, I'm asking her the name of her husband, so what's so wrong about that, huh? You know goddamn well I know everybody in the neighborhood, right? . . . *(Laughs.)* Hell, I probably know the son-of-a-bitch!

(To SONIA) Hey, don't pay him any attention, lady, he's just a kid, and when it comes to women he never could pull it off. No offense intended, kiddo, just stating the facts. I remember one time when we were younger? Jimmy dug a hole in his bedroom wall right next to mine, paper thin walls, you know? Easy as pie. Only thing is, after he got through, he realized the hole came out right behind my dresser. The kid never was very good at math.

JIMMY *(fed up, going into the kitchen)*: Oh, Christ!

JOCK: But guess what. For years he's claimed he dug the hole right where he wanted to. *(Snickers.)* O' course after that he had to go drill another right through my dresser. *(toward the kitchen)* Remember that, Jimmy?

(To SONIA*)* Then, when one of those hot little numbers'd call me up for a visit, he'd dash into my room, fling open the doors of the dresser to get a good angle, you know, a clear view. And ya know, one time he even tried to take the doors off 'n hide 'em in the cellar. *(Chuckles.)* Back in those days everybody'd go down in the cellar. *(Drinks.)* I gotta admit, I hadda put his nose outta joint a few times, ya know? Like right before. . . we'd start to do it. . . if you get my drift. (SONIA *complies with a smile.)* What I'd do, I'd start getting her clothes off, see, and soon as things started to get, well let's say. . . ya know, a little hot. . . I'd hang a towel right over that hole. Sometimes I even used her panties. *(toward the kitchen)* 'member, JIMMY? *(chuckling)* And then, I'd go on about my business.

(JIMMY *comes back from the kitchen.)* You get what I'm sayin', right? I just know you're a smart lady. *(Takes a swig.)* Jimmy never could figure out how to make the ladies dance. Jimmy'd take his buddies into his room.

JIMMY: Okay, Jock, that's enough!

JOCK: Supposedly, to peep through the hole. *(chuckling).* But what he's really up to is touchy-feely. Jimmy always had lots and lots of luck with the boys!

JIMMY: I'm telling you, Jock, you better shut up!

JOCK *(more aggressive)*: But then I always did think he was queer. *(Slight pause; he feigns a cough, as if remembering).* Ah, those were the days! Gone is the time when I'd sweep the ladies right off their feet. Quite the lady-killer, I was, too, miss, if I don't say so. But you gotta be intact, you know, to sweep a lady off her feet. To be intelligent, now, you don't need to be intact. But to sweep 'em off their feet, it's essential, absolutely essential. *(Drinks.)* And the real pisser is, women don't care diddley squat about intelligence. *(Goes over to the bar and pours another drink.)* Love turns to pity. *(He chuckles and takes a drink.)* Tell you what, though. Next woman takes pity on my leg's gonna piss blood with her teeth rammed down her throat! So! Here's to you! *(He lifts his glass and drinks. Slight pause. JIMMY seems more and more ill at ease.)* Hey, kid!

JIMMY *(wearily)*: What?

JOCK: That explosion last night? That was no explosion.

JIMMY: I know.

JOCK *(to SONIA)*: Just a little bitty earthquake, nothin' much to talk about. 'Bout three quarters of the houses around here came down, and I expect we'll be getting a visit or two. *(Drinks.)* By the way, Jimmy, I meant to remind you: this ain't no hotel, okay buddy? I know you got a soft heart, but I'm the one gives the orders aroun' here.

JIMMY *(to SONIA)*: You must be getting hungry, can I get you something to eat?

20

SONIA: No, thanks, Jimbo, I'll be fine.

JOCK *(to* JIMMY*)*: The first person comes in here asking for hospitality, do me a favor, will ya? Give him a coupla swift kicks in the gut for me, 'kay Jimmy? Myself, I can't anymore. Then shove him right out the window. *(Takes a drink.)* I won't have any stray dogs skulkin' around this house. *(Pours himself another.)*

JIMMY *(trying to change the subject)*: Sonia brought us some food.

JOCK *(With fake astonishment and mechanical compliments)*: Really! I am so very touched and moved. Bravo. *(to* SONIA, *after a pause)*

May we know what it is?

SONIA *(coldly)*: Of course. Some corn and some onions.

JOCK *(look of wonderment)*: Corn!?. . . And onions, too?! My god, are we gonna have ourselves a feast! *(Chuckles.)*

JIMMY: She also brought some ham.

JOCK: No! Really? Ham? Tell me, no really, it takes some real doing to scrape up some ham in the times we live in. Bravo! Only thing is, speaking personally of course, I think it's shit meat and I can't stand the stuff.

(to SONIA*)* But don't you worry, Jimmy'll get a kick out of eating my share. *(Drinks.)* Don't know why, but I never have liked pigs. They'll eat any goddamn thing. Worst of all, they stink like shit. For that matter I don't like eggs either.

SONIA: Don't worry, I didn't bring any eggs.

JOCK: Terrific! Thank you very much!

*(*JOCK *rapidly sips his drink. As* JIMMY *goes to pour himself another, he looks at* SONIA *who motions that she has enough.)*

You live in these parts?

SONIA: Yes.

JOCK: Far away?

SONIA: No, not very.

JOCK *(looking her over)*: And. . .'scuse my asking. . . but just what is it brings you here?

SONIA: I already told you.

JOCK: Oh? I must not have understood.

SONIA: I came to see my husband.

JOCK: No kidding! So that's it, is it? Your little shack comes crashing down, and you suddenly get this craving to come see good ol' Jimmy. Am I right?

SONIA: I'm awfully sorry to disappoint you, Jock, but my house is doing just fine. I came for another reason.

JOCK *(snickering)*: Oh, really now?

JIMMY *(after a pause)*: Jock, Sonia is moving back in with us.

(Slight pause as everyone glances at each other. JOCK still chuckles.)

I hope you don't see any inconvenience in it for you. *(very slight pause)* Because anyway it won't make the slightest bit of difference.

JOCK *(raising his voice)*: What's that you say? *(slight pause)* Inconvenience!? You must be kidding! Why, this is wonderful news!

JIMMY *(after a brief hesitation)*: That's great. I'm happy you see it this way.

JOCK: I'm happy too.

JIMMY: The only thing I'd ask is, to try and not complicate things for her.

JOCK *(at once)*: Do you realize what you're saying, Jimmy? You realize the reputation you're spreading about me? Sonia, I apologize, sincerely. You know, kid, that kind of joke makes a bad impression, and I certainly don't need your advice. Okay? So stop clowning around!

(to SONIA, a little more calmly) Would you care for a drink?

SONIA *(playing his game)*: I don't mind if I do. Whatever you're drinking.

JOCK: Jimmy, get her a drink, will you?

*(*JIMMY *does.)*

What a pleasure it is for me to welcome you into this home, you're going to brighten my days, you know. *(Drinks.)* Remember those domino games we used to play, a while back?

SONIA: It hasn't been so long, really.

JOCK: My, how time does fly! *(Drinks.)* Some helluva games, am I right? Those were the days, huh? *(He takes another swig, and seems to savor it.)* Tell me, Sonia. . .

SONIA: Yes?

JOCK: We will play again, won't we?

SONIA *(coldly)*: Of course.

*(*JIMMY *takes a seat next to* SONIA. *After a while.)*

JOCK: So. If I understand correctly, I'm gonna have to give you two my bed and return to my old corner down there, back to my little lair. Right?

JIMMY: Keep your bed, Jock, we'll find something else.

24

JOCK: Says who? No, absolutely out of the question. You're going to take my bed and that's it, it'll give me pleasure. At your age, you need all the rest you can get, need to recoup all your sap. For us old folks, there's nothing left to recoup—no, I'm happy to have the chance to sleep on the floor. That bed's too big for half a guy like me. The bigger the bed, the lonelier the space. But in some little cranny. . . No, I prefer to stay close to the door and guard the house.

JIMMY: Will you stop!? I told you we'll get along other way.

JOCK: Ah, well, that's none of my business! It's all decided. Besides, as for getting along you'll do much better in the bed. *(Gets up.)* I gotta go see about my shells.

(He goes toward the cellar door, takes a huge key out of his pocket, unlocks the door, and turns around.)

Only one thing bothers me.

JIMMY: What's that?

JOCK *(almost mysteriously)*: You did say she was coming back to live with us, right? (JIMMY, *taken by surprise, doesn't answer.)*

Speak up, Jimmy! I'm talking to you!

JIMMY: That's exactly what we agreed.

JOCK *(with a puzzled air)*: So. . . where are her bags?

JIMMY *(disconcerted)*: Well. . .

SONIA *(interrupting him)*: I'm going to get them in a while. Unless of course there's some hurry.

JOCK: Huh? No, take your time, Sonia, take your time. *(Goes down in the basement.)*

(JIMMY and SONIA left alone, kiss each other in relief, as if they've just had a close call. Blackout.)

(Same set, a few days later. The characters are in different clothes. JOCK *and* SONIA *are playing dominoes. They scarcely look at one another during the game. Throughout the entire act,* JOCK *becomes drunker and drunker.)*

JOCK *(after thinking a while)*: I need a six. *(He thinks. Slight pause.)* I don't have a six. *(He seems to be thinking still.)* If I don't have a six, I'm fucked. There's nothing I can do. *(Thinks some more.)* One little six, and I domino. *(slight pause)*. . . whereas now. . . I don't domino. *(slight pause)* Ah, Sonia! what a pleasure these games are, with you. What a joy. *(slight pause)* And you, my sweet?

SONIA: Me what?

JOCK *(looking at her)*: You enjoy these games?

SONIA: Yes! Now play!

JOCK *(slight pause)*: Jimmy doesn't like dominoes. How's it possible not to like dominoes, huh, Sonia?

SONIA: Play!

JOCK: What an amazing game! *(He thinks.)* If you don't think about what you're doing in this game, you're screwed. *(slight pause)* Even if you do think. . . *(slight pause)*. . . and you don't have a six. . . *(slight pause)* you're still screwed. *(slight pause)* That's what I like about this game.

(Slight pause. SONIA *gets up to go pour herself another drink, keeping an eye on* JOCK *to make sure he doesn't cheat.)*

Do what you will. . . *(slight pause)*. . . if you need a six and don't have one. . . *(slight pause)*, you get it straight up the ass.*(Slight pause.* SONIA *returns to her seat.)* Your turn. I pass.

SONIA: Jock, this isn't poker! In dominoes you don't pass, you draw. Those are the rules.

JOCK: I never stop drawing, with you. Drawing my own blood.

SONIA: Maybe so, but those are the rules.

JOCK *(slight pause)*: I'm tired. I don't know why, I'm flat beat, I gotta get me a drink. *(He gets up and goes over to the bar.)* My name's not Jimmy. Jimmy, he can go days on end without a drink. *(Pours himself another.)* No wonder he's got kidney problems

SONIA: First of all he doesn't have kidney problems. Secondly, you're the one who's liable to have problems, right around the liver.

JOCK: How the hell do you know he doesn't have kidney problems?

SONIA: Because! He would've told me!

JOCK: Jimmy? Jimmy never says anything. The guy's a mystic!

(SONIA laughs at JOCK's mendacity.)

And by the way, where is he? Where has the young mystic gone?

SONIA: I think he's gone to a meeting.

JOCK: A meeting? What meeting?

SONIA: I haven't the faintest idea.

JOCK *(smiles; after a while)*: The dear little thing, he never misses his chance to make an impression. To a meeting! Now I've heard everything. This must be a very special meeting, like the kind for deaf mutes, I can well imagine him presiding over that kind. *(He chuckles.)*

SONIA *(cutting)*: Unless of course it's a meeting of cripples and amputees.

(JOCK looks at her violently, then bursts out laughing.)

JOCK *(takes a drink and comes over to her)*: You really are ravishing, Sonia.

(She goes over to the window, he joins her and starts walking around her, caressing her neck.)

You know, I've known a lot of little pearls like you, my sweet, with exactly the same skin.

(She seems utterly indifferent to what he's saying. Brief silence as he continues his caresses.)

I wonder what their skin looks like now. . . I've had some delicious times. . . *(Brief silence. She moves back, not afraid, but detached.)* Scared, Sonia? Scared of me?

(Pensive, she stares out the window panes.)

Why should you be? No reason to. I wouldn't even be able to run after you! *(Brief silence. He moves closer to her.)* I want you to trust me so much! *(He stares at her. She sighs.)*

There's just. . . just one thing I'd like, sweet. *(He turns her head with his hand.)* Let me have it, please, please let me have it, the loveliest mouth in the world.

(He starts to kiss her; she pushes him; he falls down and laughs.)

SONIA: Believe me, someday I'll let you have it only it won't be my mouth!

(She goes over to the table and starts putting away the dominoes.)

JOCK: Listen, sweet! You know that story of Harold and Marilyn?

SONIA: You really ought to go dry out somewhere.

(He gets up laughing and goes to get his drink.)

JOCK: It's the story of an ugly little boy and a beautiful little girl. One day, he falls in love with her—secretly of course, otherwise he's the laughing stock of the town. *(Takes a drink.)* The boy is really ugly, really ugly; and she is very very beautiful. All the boys in town are wild about Marilyn. Now, the boys aren't all handsome, but they're not downright ugly either. She is perfectly elegant in her beautiful dress, and every night, she changes her dress.

SONIA: No harm in that.

JOCK: . . . and changes her boyfriend.

(SONIA *smiles sardonically.*)

Everybody gives her presents. Harold, he gives her presents in secret.

SONIA *(without looking at* JOCK, *putting away the game)*: The asshole!

JOCK: 'Cause first of all, he'd be the laughing stock of the whole town, and anyway he's tried it once. One time he got the guts up to look at her at close range, at less than ten yards. She made fun of him, all the boys did too, everybody threw rocks at him and spat on him.

SONIA: You sure this wasn't Jesus?

JOCK: So he runs home to his dad in tears. With his glass eye, cauliflower nose, and elephant ears, everybody called him "radar."

SONIA *(laughing)*: I know another one.

JOCK: Hey, the idea wasn't altogether unflattering, 'cause truth is he could see things a coming a long way off. So one day the lovely Marilyn catches a virus, some kinda horrible, contagious disease like the clap, which deforms her lovely features. And there was no cure for it.

SONIA *(mocking)*: What was this, the Middle Ages?

JOCK: Shut up ya little creep.

(resuming his tale) So. Nobody in town wanted to come within a mile of her anymore. Even dogs 'd bark at her. So, she gets all teary and weepy. Then one day, there's a knock at her door. She runs to open it, and guess who's standing there: good ol' Harold, holding a bouquet of flowers.

(She sniggers.)

Off in the distance, people were no longer laughing. Marilyn takes the bouquet from Harold and dissolves in tears. She hugs him oh so tight out of sheer gratitude, but then suddenly she leaps back at the thought that she might infect him with the virus. But Harold just smiles, he's safe.

SONIA: Why, he's been vaccinated?

JOCK: Shut your fucking mouth.

(He returns to the story.)

And that's when he asked for her hand in holy matrimony.

(SONIA laughs.)

Marilyn was touched to the quick by his proposal, so touched, in fact, that she fell down dead of a heart attack right on the spot, clutching her bouquet of flowers.

SONIA: What a scream.

JOCK: So Harold goes back home to his dad, with his glass eye, his cauliflower nose, his elephant ears, and with a strange little smile playing across his lips.

SONIA: I knew it. A real maniac.

(JOCK *laughs.*)

Where'd you dig up that idiotic story?

JOCK: It is not an idiotic story, it's a true story, or at least one which could be, in the logic of things.

SONIA: One thing I do know.

JOCK: Oh?

SONIA: Yes. There's somebody you need to meet.

JOCK *(very interested)*: Ah, you going to introduce me to somebody? Who's that?

SONIA: A girlfriend of mine.

JOCK *(laughs)*: No shit. Pretty?

SONIA: Very pretty.

JOCK *(obviously very interested)*: What's her problem? *(snickering all the while)* What's she do?

SONIA: She works on certain kinds of fuses.

JOCK: An electrician?

SONIA *(shaking her head)*: Psychiatrist.

JOCK: Really now!

(Just now JIMMY *comes in. He hangs up his overcoat.)*

JIMMY: Hello, Jock. *(He goes over to* SONIA.*)* Hello, darling. *(He kisses her.)*

JOCK: Hi, kid.

JIMMY: Ah, I think I'll have a little drink.

SONIA: Let me get it for you, dear. *(She goes to the bar pours him a drink, beneath the gaze of* JOCK.*)*

JIMMY: What've you guys been up to?

SONIA: A round of dominoes. Jock was unbeatable.

JOCK: Yeah, but the high point of the day was when we got onto the subject of psychoanalysis, right Sonia?

SONIA: That's right. In fact I advised him to get involved in it as soon as possible.

JOCK *(to* JIMMY, *laughing)*: And you want to know the funniest part? She thinks I'm a crazy! She keeps wantin' to drag me off to see some bitch to check me out. What d'ya say to that, Jimmy?

JIMMY: We'll see. Might not be such a bad idea.

JOCK *(a bit miffed)*: Hey, Jimmy. You remember that little Frankie kid?

JIMMY: No.

JOCK: Course you do! Remember? The kid who always used to stand right in the middle of sewer pipes?

SONIA: What was he doing in a sewer pipe?

JOCK *(to* SONIA*)*: A bounty hunter—for rats! *(to* JIMMY*)* Little Frankie! Puny little runt with his red cap?. . . Course you do! 'Member? He hated me to step on his shoes. . .

JIMMY *(pretending to remember)*: Yeah, so what about him?

JOCK *(to* JIMMY*)*: What about him? He went to a psychiatrist, that's what.

SONIA: And?

JOCK *(to* SONIA*)*: Well the guy was never half as sick as he's been since he went into therapy.

JIMMY: I just can't picture who it is.

JOCK: Doesn't matter, Jimmy. What the hell, somebody's gobbled up your brains. (*Lifts his glass and stares at him. Meanwhile* SONIA *goes over to* JIMMY *and kisses him.*)

Anyway, I wanted to propose a toast to you both. Drink this glass to your health, in profound gratitude.

JIMMY *(astonished;* SONIA *less so)* Gratitude? Gratitude for what?

JOCK: Hmm? *(He goes to the bar to fill his glass.)* Why.
. . for everything. . . for. . . everything! For the both
of you. For all your kindness and understanding, I
just wanted to propose a toast of thanks to you both.
And I particularly wanted to thank Sonia for
brightening my days so marvelously. You know, I'm
so happy now, Sonia—what a marvelous idea you
had, inviting yourself in like that. I actually believe
that if you hadn't forced yourself on us, we would've
been forced to go out and get you.

JIMMY *(annoyed)*: If anybody around here is forcing
himself on anyone, seems to me that it's you, Jock!

JOCK: Aw, come on. What're you insinuating? I'm not
the one, it's this house has been forced on me. Don't
you forget: I bought it, paid for it with my own
dough. And keep in mind the day our old man died.

JIMMY: Please, you're not gonna start on that!

JOCK: And don't forget his last words. I can see it now.
There I was, sitting at the head of his bed; you, over
by the door in your pajamas, your face like a block
of ice; and him, with his tongue cancer, lying there
in bed, he says: "Don't forget, Jock, you're the one
gets all the dough. Okay kid? I've scrimped an'
saved all my fuckin' life for you, kid, you got that?
I've rummaged through garbage trucks for jewelry
on account that skunk, Dorval, I even played the
horses for you, Jock, you remember that, okay?
Otherwise, I'da got the hell out years ago, hopped
the first train 'n started a new life with the first
babe along. You got that, Jock? And I woulda. . . I
woulda stuffed Jimmy in a box 'n left 'im behind an
altar! Okay? I always did like to travel."

JIMMY: Screw this bullshit!

(He and SONIA *are still in each other's arms.)*

JOCK: ". . . I really woulda liked to've lived in Manhattan, maybe Rome even, or Hamburg! So okay, fuck it! The shit is, I never did leave, I was born in this fucked-up neighborhood, I grew up in this fucked-up neighborhood, and I'm gonna die in this fucked-up neighborhood. The shit is, I never had the balls to just up an' blow it off, I coulda pissed right in their faces 'n got the hell out, ya know? Only I just sat here! Not like you!" Then he grabbed me by the balls and said: "Okay, Jock? you, you're the real champ!" After that, I took off his glasses, set them down, and closed his eyes. *(He takes a drink.)*

*(*SONIA *and* JIMMY *are still kissing.)*

That was just before we found the old lady's bones out in the back yard, shoved six feet under. 'Member that, Jimmy? *(He laughs.)*

SONIA: You're not only a goddamn cheater, Jock! You're a goddamn asshole!

JOCK: Huh? What's this cheater? What are you talking? You're mixin' up everthing, Sonia! Don't listen to her, kid, let me tell you how it was: Okay. Here I was out of sixes, so I say to myself. . .

JIMMY *(interrupting)*: Save your breath, I really don't give a damn!

*(*JOCK *smiles and takes a drink.)*

JOCK *(to* SONIA*)*: In any case, Lady, I could give a shit what you think! You're a sly little slut, aren't you? A real acrobat. *(Takes another sip.)* A real little hag.

SONIA: And you, you're nothing but a one-legged puppet!

JIMMY *(to* SONIA, *as if to say it's not worth talking to him)*: Let it go, sweetheart.

JOCK *(as if* JIMMY *were taking his side)*: Relax, kid. Let her piss 'n moan. This is fun. Go ahead, sweetheart, do your thing!

(She doesn't say a word, but goes to get a drink. Jock watches her with a strange grin.)

Hey, Jimmy!

JIMMY *(detached)*: Yeah.

JOCK: How come she's not pissin' 'n moanin'?

JIMMY: Would you stop this little game? See if you can talk about something else!

JOCK *(smiling)*: That's it, that's right, let's talk about something else. Good idea! Let's drink to that. *(He raises his glass.)* Eh, Jimmy? *(*JIMMY *just looks at him.)* I propose a toast. . . *(slight pause)* Hey, Jimmy. Doncha wanna know who I'm toasting?

JIMMY: You really ought to go get some sleep, Jock.

JOCK: Sleep? I want to propose a toast, not get some sleep! Your mixin' up everything.

JIMMY: In all honesty, I really think it would do you good.

JOCK: Faggot! *(Takes a sip.)* I thought I already told you, kid. I don't need any advice from you. Okay kid? *(Drinks again. Brief silence.)* Hey, Jimmy. You know who I'm gonna propose this toast to?

JIMMY: Stop drinking!

JOCK: You little dipshit. One of these days I'm gonna make you eat your words, set that down willya! And I mean raw! *(He drinks, then goes to the bar to pour himself another, then lies down on the bed. Silence. JIMMY and SONIA go into the kitchen, then return.)*

JOCK *(after a while)*: So. How'd the meeting go?

JIMMY *(hesitantly)*: Okay.

JOCK: "Okay?" What's that supposed to mean?

JIMMY: I don't really feel like talking about it, it wasn't terribly interesting.

JOCK: Huh? What the hell are you doing at a meeting which isn't terribly interesting? The most intelligent member of the family! *(JIMMY sighs.)* I just don't know you anymore, kid. Sometimes I wonder if I'm in the right house. You never know, such things happen. You go out, knock back a few, wander over where the whores hang out, head east along the Avenue with a pint of bourbon, turn 'round, stagger back through the whores drunk as a sailor, circle around the block a couple more times, stuff yourself silly in some greasy spoon, then tank up some more 'til you make it home pissed to the gills. And guess what? You fucked up! You're in the wrong house! You've staggered right into a neighbor's house without even knowin' it, you flop down on some bed, pass out under a blanket like a stray dog, next to some old biddy, and. . . you don't even know where you live anymore, and you don't know who you are.

(He stares at his brother for several seconds.)

So what about you, huh? Who are you? *(Takes a drink.)* Your name, please?

JIMMY: Stop it, will you?

JOCK: I don't know who you are, anymore.

JIMMY: Will you stop this crap!! *(A little calmer, conciliatory, after a pause.)* It was only about dividing up some land.

JOCK: Ah! You see? that wasn't so hard, and. . . pray, what land might that be?

JIMMY: I'm talking about old man Picard's property.

JOCK *(sitting up straight, as if he'd just heard something utterly absurd)*: Who? Picard!! You mean you wanna divvy up old Jeff's land? I tell you, he's just liable to have something to say about that! Fact, I know he will. Oh no, he's not gonna appreciate that one bit! Not ol' Jeff Picard, no sirreee! Jeff's my best friend, and don't you forget that, Jimmy!

JIMMY: Jeff Picard is dead.

(They look at each other.)

JOCK: Please. Don't kid around about things like that, you hear?

JIMMY: I'm telling you. Jeff's dead.

JOCK: Where?

JIMMY *(After a pause,* JOCK *stares intently at* JIMMY.*)*: In his rocking chair.

(Brief silence. JOCK *seems sincerely moved.)*

JOCK: When? When did he die?

JIMMY: Oh, please.

JOCK: I'm asking you to tell me: when did my very own best friend die?

(They look at each other. Then, calmer.)

You're not gonna tell me he's been dead a long time.

JIMMY *(with a fatalistic air)*: Yes.

41

JOCK *(still quite moved)*: How long? How long, Jimmy?

JIMMY: Several years now.

(Brief silence. JOCK has a drink.)

JOCK: And. . . what did he die of?

JIMMY: Old age.

JOCK *(calmly)*: You tryin' to fuck with my brain, or what? *(He recoils.)* Old age!! What are you two up to, eh? *(Glares at them.)* Jeff Picard was younger than I am!!

JIMMY: Don't be silly. The man was at least ninety-five.

JOCK: You sure? *(JIMMY nods.)* Are you absolutely sure of this, Jimmy?

JIMMY: Of course I'm sure! What's gotten into you?

JOCK: Hmmm? Oh, nothing. No, what you just said makes me feel better. *(He takes a drink, the others stare at him.)* Funny, no one ever told me.

JIMMY: But you're the one who placed a wreath on his grave!

JOCK: A wreath? Me? I placed a wreath? *(Takes a drink. Brief silence.)*

42

For that low-down scumbag son-of-bitch?! That stinking piece of fish shit? His father had the smelliest goddamn fish-stand on the whole planet! *(He takes a drink, then, as if he had never known him, and as if completely indifferent to his death:)* Who was the guy, anyway?

SONIA *(entering into the spirit, but with a weary air)*: You just said it: a low-down scumbag!

JOCK *(to JIMMY)*: Ah. So that's it, is it. You're gonna split up his land?

JIMMY: Yeah.

JOCK: That's great, that's really good, really good. Only thing is, it's all a little bit rocky, isn't it, his land?

JIMMY: That was precisely one of the main points of the discussion.

JOCK: Tell me, kid. Since when did you know shit about the field of agriculture?

JIMMY: Oh, I think I know enough to know you can't grow a head of cabbage on a slab of concrete.

JOCK: Oh really, now, you really believe that, you little jerk-off? Okay, I'll make you a bet. I'll bet you that I can grow a dozen head right here in this room—that's right, kid, make 'em grow right here on the spot, and then you'll see. When it comes to agriculture, I'm at the top of the field. I been growin' cabbage heads for goin' on thirty years.

SONIA: Well, I must say, it suits you—even if it hasn't done much for you.

JOCK: Nice, very nice. You really are sharp, you know. Maybe not the personification of kindness, but. . . sharp.

SONIA: Thanks, Jock. You, on the other hand, are very kind.

(He takes a drink.)

JOCK: I know I'm a kind person. What can I do? it's my nature.

(He empties his glass. SONIA goes over to JIMMY and kisses him. Brief silence.)

But nature has its limits.

(He watches them kiss.)

Limits which are undiscovered, by the way. *(Brief silence.)* I wanna drink.

(Pause. They don't hear him.)

I'm thirsty. Having a drink when you're thirsty, no harm in that. Kind? You bet I am, but you gotta stay within the limits. *(No response.)* Just because I'm kind doesn't mean I'm not thirsty.

(JIMMY tries to free himself from SONIA's embrace to serve JOCK, but SONIA holds him back.)

SONIA: Wait a minute, darling, just one more little kiss.

JOCK *(mockingly, a little annoyed)*: One more little kiss, I missed you, missed kiss, kiss missed.

(She kisses him again.)

The day will come when I've had enough, on that day, I guarantee, you'll see what I can do!

(She continues to cling to JIMMY.*)*

JIMMY *(managing to free himself)*: You want a scotch?

JOCK: Of course I want a scotch, you moron! What else would I want but a scotch!

SONIA: Jock, you really shouldn't. You're already completely smashed.

JIMMY *(to* SONIA, *with a little accommodating smile)*: Lay off, sweetheart.

JOCK: What's that you say, Jimmy?

JIMMY *(serving him)*: I wasn't talking to you.

JOCK: So I'm drunk, am I?

JIMMY: I didn't say that.

JOCK: You must think I'm an idiot.

JIMMY *(turning to* SONIA*)*: Enough. . . I'm tired.

JOCK: Tired? What have you done to get tired?

JIMMY: Stop it.

JOCK: Stop what?

JIMMY *(calmly)*: Shit!

(JIMMY and SONIA start kissing again.)

JOCK *(takes a drink; after a moment)*: Can't even carry on a decent conversation anymore in this shit-hole. *(brief silence)* Will you stop that for god's sake!? *(Slight pause. He takes a drink.)* I haven't said anything for a while now, here I am, lying down, and I haven't said a word. *(slight pause)* I told you to see a doctor, Jimmy. . . *(brief silence)* 'stead of shoving it in my face! I don't see why you two have to stick it to me. *(Takes a drink.)* Here I am, minding my own business, not a peep outta me, while you, you two gang up and stomp me into the dirt!

JIMMY *(between two kisses)*: Who's stomping on you, Jock?

(During this speech, JIMMY and SONIA are continuously kissing, evidently not hearing him at all.)

JOCK: You are! Trampling all over me! I see through your game though. *(He drinks.)* You're tryin' to beat me down, aren't ya, trample me down like a herd of buffalo. *(He snorts derisively.)* Agh! You're wastin' your time. Look at this neck, willya? Look at these swollen veins. *(Snickers, more and more drunkenly)* Nobody could slice these open. *(Takes a drink.)* Veins o' steel. Look at that! You'd break a knife on that! *(Slight pause. JIMMY and SONIA pay no attention.)* Go ahead and laugh! *(Drinks.)* I'm the buffalo here! An' you? You're nothin' but a coupla piss ants. *(slight pause)* Talk, goddammit! Say somethin'! If a guy can't talk unner his own roof, where can he? *(Takes a swig.)* I ain't by god gonna start talkin' to myself out in the streets, folks starin' at me like a dog, no thank you! *(Snickers.)* Oh no, oh no. I won't give you that pleasure. *(Takes a drink.)* I'm no fuckin' lunatic!

(JIMMY goes over to the bar, pours himself a drink, comes back to SONIA, then turns to JOCK.)

JIMMY *(JOCK appears thoughtful)*: While I'm thinking about it. *(He digs in his pocket.)* I brought you a little something. *(He hands a sea shell to JOCK.)* For you, JOCK.

JOCK *(He takes the shell, sits down on the bed, wide-eyed with wonder)*: Where did you find this? It's wonderful, the most beautiful shell I've ever seen in my entire life. *(He looks at it closer.)* Where'd you find it?

JIMMY: Down in Norman's basement.

JOCK: In Norman's basement? *(He stares at the shell.)* Thanks, kid, it's magnificent. *(Drinks.)* This'll make the prettiest in my whole collection.

(JIMMY returns to SONIA. JOCK continues to examine the shell.)

Hey, Jimmy?

JIMMY: Yes?

JOCK: What the hell were you doin' down in Norman's basement?

JIMMY: Nothing, he was showing me his equipment.

JOCK *(after a second)*: What equipment?

JIMMY: His fishing equipment!

JOCK *(looking back down at his shell)*: You sure it wasn't some other equipment?

JIMMY: What's that supposed to mean?

JOCK: Oh, nothing. Just thought I'd ask.

(He takes a drink. JIMMY too.)

JIMMY *(after a second)*: He wants us to go fishing next week, he even invited you.

JOCK: What, with that trash?

JIMMY: Don't say that.

JOCK: I say he's a goddamn pig fucker. The guy knows I can't stand water! Or maybe the idea is to throw me overboard, huh? What he forgets though, he doesn't know how to swim either!

(JIMMY *and* SONIA *grin.* JOCK *takes a drink.*)

So what were you doin' down there with Norman, eh Jimmy?

JIMMY *(still amused)*: Jock, come on.

JOCK: I won't have you goin' down in Norman's basement. Okay? Answer me!

(SONIA *and* JIMMY *kiss each other again.*)

What's this fishing shit? I don't imagine you two went down there for some other reason? Don't think I'm a total fool. *(He drinks.)* You know what I think? I think you two went down there for some touchy-feely! *(He laughs.)*

JIMMY *(coldly)*: Very funny. You're just full of wit these last few days, truly a charm.

JOCK *(looking at the shell)*: In any case, thanks for the shell, kid, it is absolutely splendid, a stroke of luck that, Norman takin' you down in his basement. *(Drinks.)* Really splendid.

(SONIA *goes to pour herself a drink, slowly.*)

49

Reminds me of a specimen I found in a wreck once off the side of the road, where there'd been a crash. Almost the same, not the color, but the shape. *(Looks thoughtful.)* I remember I didn't take it with me, I just left it there in the car.

JIMMY: Why's that?

JOCK *(lost in thought)*: Mmm?

JIMMY: Why did you leave it in the car?

JOCK: Because of the blood.

JIMMY: What blood?

JOCK: The blood! It was all bloodstained.

JIMMY: What do you mean?

JOCK: What do you mean what do I mean? With all the dead bodies in that car, you'd expect it to be a little bloody, I think.

JIMMY: Bodies? What dead bodies? You never told me about this.

JOCK *(trying not to go into it)*: Eh? 'bout what?

JIMMY *(looking at him askance)*: What's all this about dead bodies? What happened?

JOCK: What happened? Nothing at all happened—they were all dead!

(JIMMY and SONIA give JOCK a strange look. He drinks.)

What're you lookin' at me like that for? I'm tellin' you they were already dead. Already dead when I got to the car. *(He takes a swig.)* Fact, they were dead before I got to the car. The driver looked like a maniac—the kind you see on holidays. My guess is he didn't see the tree an' smashed right into it. *(Takes a drink.)* In fact, he wrapped the whole front end aroun' that tree.

SONIA: How many were there in the car?

JOCK *(trying to minimize the affair)*: Huh? Oh, only four, four at the most.

JIMMY: Did you call the police?

JOCK: What for? To get grilled three days and nights straight with a lamp in my eyes, like some terrorist? *(imitating an interrogation)* What time was it? Were you at the scene of the accident when it happened? What were you doing there? Weren't you in the middle of the road?

(to JIMMY*)* Okay, let's have it! *(slight pause.)* I was hunting mushrooms! *(louder)* You don't hunt mushrooms in the middle of a highway! *(calmer)* I started with the woman. She felt cold. Then I lit my lighter, 'cause it was just then aroun' nightfall, and I saw the maniac behind the wheel, he was dead too, then I looked in the back seat and there was this like grandmother with pink hair or somethin', and. . . and a little boy who was holding a seashell. I looked at the little boy, then I looked at the shell, and then I put it back in his hand. *(He drinks.)*

JIMMY: Are you sure they were dead?

JOCK: Asshole. Were they dead, he asks. They don't come any deader, kid! Were they dead he asks me, me, who's worked over three weeks in the biggest morgue in the country! If you'd seen the number of corpses I've seen, you'd be at the hospital right now for eye surgery.

JIMMY: You've never had eye surgery, as far I know.

JOCK: That's cause I'm not a softy! *(Takes a large swig. The following monologue to be delivered with animation, and with mounting violence.)*

Besides, who says I never called the police? Wanna know something? I did, I did call the police, and I said to them: "Listen to me you buncha jerkoffs, there's a dead drunk wrapped aroun' a tree out on highway 35 'bout two miles up from Black Cat Tavern—drunk as a hoot-owl more 'n likely. Thing is, the guy took the whole family out for a drive, didn't spot that tree out there on 35 and ran smack right into it, so now what you got for the last three four hours is four more dead bodies out there on 35, ya understan', assholes? So it might be a good idea for you to get up off your fat butts, run out there and scrape up the bodies, ya know? Frankly, it doesn't make a very good impression, out there on the side of the road!"

(JIMMY and SONIA look at each other, amazed at this speech. JOCK has a drink, as if nothing had happened. Then, calmly.)

Then I hung up. *(slight pause)* How easy it is to change the subject.

(JOCK is clearly getting a little drunk.)

JIMMY: What's this you're saying?

JOCK: There's something's been buggin' me, Jimmy.

JIMMY: Oh? What's bugging you?

JOCK: I'd like to know what the hell you were doing down there in Norman's cellar!

JIMMY: Oh, please, let's not start that again.

JOCK: I'd like to know who I'm living with in this house, that's all.

JIMMY *(wearily)*: It's so boring.

JOCK *(laughs)*: Which of you two was the woman, Jimmy?

SONIA: Oh, go get fucked!

JOCK *(laughing)*: Who, me? No, I meant, between Jimmy and Norman, which was the woman—I wasn't talkin' about me. Sonia, you know very well that you and I, we were, we were playing dominoes while Jimmy and Norman were. . . swopping fish stories. No, really. What I'd like to know is this: which of you two got humped—that's what really intrigues me. *(He laughs. JIMMY gulps down his drink and starts to put on his overcoat.)*

SONIA *(following him)*: Honey! don't listen to him, don't go, Jimmy, he's drunk!

(JIMMY leaves, slamming the door behind him. She turns to JOCK furious.)

You happy now, you bastard!?

JOCK: Happy? No, no, I'm not at all! Look Sonia I just wanna to know if I'm livin' with one woman or two in this shithole, that's all. Hey, I know the guy's a fairy, that's not the problem, that's not what's botherin' me. What I want to know is. . . which of the two fairies does he represent? *(He splutters with laughter.)*

SONIA: You really are sick! Anyway, for you, there's only one alternative.

JOCK *(Stops laughing. Strangely, he holds up his hands.)*: That's where you're wrong, Sonia that's where you're wrong. I still have a few arguments.

SONIA *(bursts out laughing, almost happy)*: Arguments? What arguments? What arguments do you mean?

(He holds up his hands.)

Those aren't arguments—they lack sap, you're completely devoid of it, Jock you understand? You have no more sap!

(She shrinks away from him as if he were contagious.)

You're like a rotten tree, a putrid, rotten tree with only one desire: to infect the whole forest. But you're wasting your time, Jock. We're still alive, whereas you, you're dead, you're already dead!

(She exits as JOCK snickers. Blackout.)

(Several days later. JIMMY *and* SONIA *are having breakfast.* JOCK *is out. They're wearing different clothes, and the little portable radio is playing jazz. Outside, it's raining rather heavily, and the noise of the rain beating on the windowpanes is heard, along with the occasional sound of thunder, as yet muffled and distant.)*

JIMMY *(finishing his breakfast)*: What a delicious breakfast!

(They smile. JIMMY *pours himself some more coffee.)*

Got any more of that ham?

SONIA *(getting up to clear the dishes)*: Nope, not a single slice. Somebody ate it all. *(going into the kitchen)* You'd think there was wolf here. *(She goes out and comes back immediately.)* It's kinda scary, holding a beast like that in your arms. *(She smiles. She sits down on his lap and they kiss. After several seconds,* SONIA *lifts her head at a sudden clap of thunder.)*

I'm scared, Jim, hold me tight.

JIMMY *(hugging her close)*: Don't be silly, dear. I'm right here.

SONIA *(looking out the window with a troubled, pensive air)*: It isn't the storm that bothers me, it's the dark. Why is it always so dark?

JIMMY: I don't know, dear. Try not to think about it. I'm sure everything'll be all right.

(They hug each other.)

I hope I'll be able to go to the meeting.

SONIA: Are you crazy? don't you see what's going on out there?

JIMMY *(smiling)*: It'll probably settle down, don't worry.

SONIA: You'll be the only one there. Nobody's going out in this weather.

JIMMY *(playfully putting his finger on the tip of her nose)*: You're wrong, the others just live a few doors down from the hall. I'll go out soon as it slacks up.

SONIA *(with a girlish, pouty look)*: Darling, I have to confess something to you.

(JIMMY looks at her.)

Jock was right about my house.

JIMMY *(with a tender smile)*: Don't think twice about it, my dear. Anyway, I knew all about it.

SONIA *(teasingly)*: And you didn't say a word!

JIMMY: Can I make a confession too?

SONIA: Oooh, tell me, tell me, what's the big secret?

JIMMY: I'm glad that house collapsed.

(She gives him a teasing little tap on the shoulder.)

SONIA: That's not a very nice thing to say!

JIMMY: Otherwise you might not be here, and I feel so happy with you around.

SONIA: Michael asked me to stay at his place, but I said no, I'd rather be with you.

(They look at each other affectionately.)

JIMMY: I guess he's still telling you to get a divorce.

SONIA: No, not this time. All he said was, I could stay with him as long as I liked, and I could help him with the farm if I wanted to. . . *(She kisses his forehead.). . .*but I couldn't do it. *(They look at each other a long while.)* And I asked him to drive me here.

JIMMY: And he didn't say anything?

SONIA: No. Fact is, he didn't have anything to say. *(She smiles.)* His face became very grave, almost sad, and that's really only thing that might've bothered me. *(She kisses his forehead.)* Then, he went and he got me a bag of groceries. *(She kisses him again.)* and he let me off at your door. *(They hug.)*

JIMMY *(tenderly)*: I love you, my darling.

(Long silence.)

SONIA: Sweetheart. . . there's something else I have to tell you.

(A loud clap of thunder.)

JIMMY: What's that?

SONIA *(She seems very embarrassed.)*: I. . . I've got a problem.

JIMMY *(surprised and worried)*: But. . . what's wrong?

SONIA: I think. . . that I'm going to have a problem staying here.

JIMMY *(incredulous)*: What's this?

SONIA: I mean. . . I'm having a problem staying in this house. *(They look at each other.)* I. . . I didn't quite know how to broach the subject.

JIMMY *(He slides her off his knees and goes over to the window. After a moment.)*: It's because of him, isn't it?

SONIA: Yes. *(brief silence)* I have a lot of trouble putting up with him. *(brief silence)* I hesitated a long long time before I came back. *(Brief silence. We hear the sound of the rain beating against the windowpanes.)* If he hadn't been here, I would've come back long before. *(brief silence)* As a matter of fact, I never would've left. *(Brief silence. JIMMY seems sad and embarrassed.)*

JIMMY: Darling. . . *(He's still staring out the window.)* He's my brother. He's not really a bad guy, he's just. . . unhappy. *(brief silence)* I know it's hard not to take his behavior at face value, but. . .

SONIA *(turning her back)*: I'll say it's hard, and you of all people should know that, right?

JIMMY: Sweetheart, listen—it's almost as if you weren't aware of his situation. *(slight pause)* If it hadn't been for that stupid accident, he'd be the Jock he always was—really a great guy.

(SONIA *laughs nervously, but softly.)* If only I hadn't left that thing at the foot of the stairs!

SONIA *(vigorously)*: Jimmy, it wasn't your fault! *(Silence. The sound of the rain.)*

JIMMY *(with a sad smile)* No wonder all the girls in the neighborhood lined up outside his bedroom. *(He laughs, almost nervously. Slight pause.)* He had something extra. A fantastic sort of gaiety. . . *(slight pause)* Everybody was attracted to him, as if drawn by. . . by some kind of power. . .

SONIA *(moving closer to* JIMMY, *gently)*: Darling, he isn't the Jock he used to be. This one is no good.

JIMMY: Don't say that, Sonia.

SONIA: He despises you. *(*JIMMY *stares intently at her.)* He has no consideration for you, he does everything he can to destroy you, and you, during it all, you wallow in guilt over that scythe you left lying around by accident!

JIMMY *(taking her by the shoulders)*: Sonia! We've got to help him.

SONIA: My poor sweet dear! *(She goes over to the bar and pours herself a drink.)* I've been thinking about something for several days now. You know that tower on the lake?

JIMMY: Sure, where they treat radiation victims, right?

SONIA: Right, but that's not all they do, they have other services: dermatology, cardiology, psychiatry, a cancer ward, and so on. *(slight pause)* They also have a maternity ward, and an old folks' home, I think. *(slight pause)* I had a chance to visit the center with Miss Dideaux, you know, the ex-schoolteacher. . .*(slight pause)* We were quite surprised by their facilities. Inside, everything is ultra-modern. *(slight pause)* Each patient has his own private nurse, entirely at his disposal. . . *(slight pause)* and the equipment available is remarkably tailored to each patient. *(Slight pause. JIMMY is still looking out at the rain.)* You want a drink?

JIMMY *(turning to SONIA)*: Please, I'll have a scotch.

(She pours him a drink and brings it over.)

SONIA: They also have a service for. . . for the disabled.

(They look at each other as they drink.)

JIMMY: Sonia! There's no way Jock's going into that kind of hospital. *(Slight pause. They drink.)* Okay, I'm willing to admit he's not totally in his right mind, but. . . he is my brother.

(glancing at SONIA) Right?

SONIA *(going over to him)*: And what about me, Jimmy? What am I in this situation?

JIMMY *(taking her in his arms)*: You?. . . You're my
wife. . . and I love you more than anything. *(slight
pause)* But I don't want to put Jock away, not in
that place.

*(SONIA's eyes flash and she frees herself from his
embrace. Silence.)*

SONIA: I think. . . I think it's about time you knew the
truth. *(slight pause)*

JIMMY: The truth about what?

(She drinks in silence.)

The truth about what, sweetheart?

*(Just now, JOCK comes in, with his cane and a
backpack.)*

JOCK: Goddamn fucking son-of-a bitch!

JIMMY: What's the matter, Jock!

JOCK: Huh? You askin' me what's the matter? You got
a nerve. I just about get myself zapped by lightning
about twenty times and you ask me what's the
matter? You're really something, you. *(He takes off
his gear.)* I'm practically drowning and he asks me
what's the matter. *(He chuckles.)* You got a great
sense of humor, Jimmy. Gimme a drink, willya?

(JIMMY goes to get him a drink. After a moment.)
Hello, Lady. *(She doesn't answer. JIMMY brings the
drink.)* Hey, Jimmy. Why didn't you tell me?

JIMMY: Tell you? Tell you about what?

JOCK: What do you mean, what? That she's *deaf*, for chrissake! *(He takes a drink.)* And those dirty little brats at me again, pokin' their sticks in the spokes. *(Drinks.)* What the fuck are they doin' out in that rain, anyway? *(Drinks.)* There I was spread-eagled with my head right in the gutter. *(Drinks.)* Lucky thing that dwarf was in the neighborhood!

JIMMY *(amazed)*: Dwarf? What dwarf?

JOCK: "What dwarf?" A dwarf! A little bitty dwarf, and what the fuck he was doing there I'll never know. But there he was. Some kinda dwarf, how do I know what dwarf? all I know is, the cretin ripped out about half my hair.

JIMMY: Oh? And what was the occasion?

JOCK: On the occasion of my drowning! I don't dare look if I got any left.

SONIA: I bet you insulted him.

JOCK: Hah? What—was I supposed to thank him? The guy rips half the scalp outta my skull and I'm supposed to kiss his ass?

SONIA: Take a look in the mirror, Jock. Truth is, you didn't have much to lose.

JOCK: You know something, Sonia? Some day you're gonna lick my boots!

(SONIA snorts derisively. After a moment.)

JIMMY: Where did you go?

JOCK *(With a curious glance)*: And you? You two get your rocks off? That's the main thing, isn't it, getting your rocks off? Well I didn't get off. I went to see Morgan.

JIMMY: What, the seed man?

JOCK *(drinks)*: Never could stand the guy, gives me the creeps. He's like a pear turned upside down. And I hate pears. *(Takes a drink.)* On the other hand, he's got good seeds. I don't know where he finds 'em, but they're damn good.

SONIA: Next thing you know he'll have us growing his cabbages.

(The rains stops.)

JOCK: That's exactly what I intend to do, Lady. In a week 'n a half we'll have cabbages sprouting right here in this living-room—a brand new hybrid. *(He takes a drink.)* I'm gonna turn this room into a little garden—from now on we'll live in a garden, right kid?

JIMMY: Sure, whatever you want. Only this isn't any construction site, okay?

JOCK: Who's talking about a construction site? What construction site? I'm talking about a little garden, not a construction site. Now wouldn't you enjoy that, Madame, a little garden?

SONIA: Would I! I hope you build us a few columns, too.

JOCK *(with a roguish look)*: Columns?! What columns? What kind of columns are you trying to suggest, Sonia?

SONIA *(a little irked)*: Whatever. I don't give a damn.

JOCK *(chuckles)*: That's what I like about you, Sonia your imagination. It may be a little twisted, but nevertheless it's real. I never would've thought of planting columns in a living-room. Not a bad idea.

(He stretches out on the bed, with a thoughtful air. SONIA is drinking her orange juice. A loud clap of thunder is heard, but the rain has stopped. To himself:) Columns!

(He laughs softly. JIMMY, until now by the window, goes over by the door, puts on a jacket, then a big overcoat, and a slicker.)

JIMMY *(going over to SONIA and taking her in his arms):* I'm going now, it's stopped raining.

JOCK: Columns, for chrissake!

(While SONIA and JIMMY kiss, JOCK gets up and goes to the bar to pour a drink.)

JIMMY: See you tonight, darling.

SONIA *(a little annoyed at his leaving)*: Right. See you tonight, take care of yourself.

(He kisses her again and goes out.)

JIMMY *(as he is leaving, without looking round)*: Bye, Jock.

(No answer. JOCK *seems not to hear or see* JIMMY *leave. He sits down in the rocking chair. A moment or two pass.* SONIA, *by the window, goes to the bar to pour a scotch.)*

JOCK *(snickering)*: Antique columns, with gladiators!

(SONIA looks at him, surprised.)

What do you think of that, my dear? Would you like gladiators?

SONIA *(a little taken back)*: Why not?

JOCK: With all their nets 'n pitchforks 'n clubs, 'n. . . Lady?

SONIA: Yes?

JOCK: Where could we find some gladiators?

SONIA: Well. . . I suppose that needs a little thought.

JOCK: Okay, let's think on it. *(Takes a drink.)* But if we find gladiators, we have to get lions, too, right, Lady? Without lions, our gladiators'll be bored stiff.

SONIA: Let's see. . . They'd still have the opportunity to beat each other up. Ah! I've got it, I bet you would make an excellent gladiator!

JOCK: Huh? Yes, an excellent idea. I'm sure I could be a good fighter.

SONIA: Of course you could. And then we could always say that your leg was gnawed off by a lion, right? What do you think?

65

JOCK: Very intelligent, Sonia very. But who would be the lion? Apart from you, sweetheart, I don't see anybody. And of course you roar so beautifully when you want. And 'm not even talkin' about your big teeth. Sure, it'd be child's play. Come on, show me your teeth, sweetheart! Just to make sure they're not really a horse's! *(He laughs.)*

SONIA: You know what you remind me of, Jock? *(He has no time to answer.)* A completely degenerate shit-fly.

JOCK *(smiling)*: I find you very intelligent, darling—not very polite, but so intelligent! Sometimes I have to wonder what the fuck you're doing with your emotional life, like what the fuck are you doing with Jimmy? Turning him spoiled rotten on me, that's what.

(SONIA looks at him, perplexed. She takes a drink.)

SONIA: What I can't figure is who invented you. . .

(JOCK chuckles.)

Not really a horrible disease. Not really an animal either. Well, maybe a crab- louse—yeah, that's it—some sort of mutant. . . crab-louse.

JOCK *(laughing louder and louder)*: I really get a kick out of you, sweetheart. You want to know somethin'? You may be a dumb little cunt, but I like having you around.

(Laughs and takes a drink. SONIA doesn't bother answering. After a while, their eyes meet and they

stare at one another. The rain starts falling again and can be heard beating against the windowpanes.)

SONIA *(After a while)*: Is there something you want?

JOCK: Who me? No.

SONIA: So why are you staring at me?

JOCK: Sweetheart, I'm not *staring* at you, I'm devouring you with my eyeballs.

SONIA: Right—that's what bothers me!

JOCK: I'm digging around inside you.

SONIA *(a flash of lightning)*: Ah hah!

JOCK: Yeah. I dig and I dig and the more I dig, the messier it gets. You know, it ain't easy diggin' around inside you—it's a real cess-pool down there! It's all buried deep down inside, but how long do you think you can hide it? You know? it's true, sometimes I gotta wonder.On the surface, everything looks rosy, everything's smooth, but underneath? . . . *(brief silence)*

SONIA: I know what you want.

JOCK: Oh? But I don't want anything, do I look like I want anything? Apart from a drink, I can't see what I could want.

SONIA: I suppose you'd want me to get that for you, too.

JOCK: Would you, sweet?

(She goes to get him his drink. Silence. A thunderclap.)

I love these cozy little evenings at home with you. Being with you just fills me with joy, that's the truth, I really get off on you.

SONIA *(bringing his drink)*: Just don't get off too much, lover.

JOCK: No, no, not too much, just what's right. By god I count myself lucky, though. Hell, I could've fallen in with a sex maniac instead of you, right sweetheart? No in all seriousness, you have a remarkable sense of humour, sparkling, refined, maybe just a little on the perverted side, but, no I'm really lucky, and of course I love you so much sometimes it. . .

SONIA *(fed up)*: Bullshit!

(He looks at her for several seconds with a pained air.)

JOCK: Feeling sad, sweet? Don't be like that. I hate it when you're sad. Be gay, not sad! 'sides, there's no reason to be! You've got two men in this house completely bonkers for you. Jimmy loves you like a fool, and as far as I'm concerned you're my very own little precious pearl. And Jimmy absolutely treasures you. You're held in high esteem here, precious. In our house, you are highly valued, never forget that.

SONIA *(coldly)*: Some day I'm going to kill you.

JOCK *(laughing)*: Don't say things like that, precious. It gives me a hard on. *(laughing)* As you know, we only kill the ones we love.

(She puts down her drink, walks around behind him and takes the shotgun down off the wall.)

SONIA *(with a machiavellian smile)*: You're right, my love, you're absolutely right.

(She puts the shotgun to his head.)

JOCK *(feeling the barrel, slightly awkward)*: What are you doing, Lady.

SONIA: I love you!

JOCK: Ah. So get that thing off my head.

SONIA: Why?

JOCK: Because! You hold the damn thing like a broomstick! *(Laughs.)*

SONIA: You said it yourself: we only kill the ones we love.

JOCK *(laughing, a bit nervously)*: Which is why, with you, I got no problem.

SONIA *(in the light of a lightning flash, she is cold and calm)*: That's where you're wrong, you've made a slight miscalculation. I only think of you, even at night, I can't sleep thinking about you.

JOCK: What's this bullshit? *(He laughs a bit stiffly.)*

SONIA *(cold and calm)*: This is no bullshit. I'm madly in love with you!

JOCK *(voice rising)*: You stupid fuck, what're you raving about? Little bitch—you never could stand the sight of me!

SONIA: Not true!

JOCK: Well then I'll never understand shit about women. Even as a kid you couldn't stand the sight of me!

SONIA: So what made you so insistent?

JOCK: Me, I was insistent?

SONIA: That's right. You were insistent. Which is why I'm going to blow your brains out.

JOCK: You never loved me. And couldn't stand it when I made a pass.

SONIA: That's the truth. I couldn't stand it.

JOCK: Ah! You see?

SONIA: So why were you always making a pass?

JOCK: Fuck. I dunno. Had to pass the time somehow.

SONIA *(with a cold intent stare)*: Like I say: you're a real sweetheart of a. . . creep. You're right. I couldn't shoot you, you're too disgusting. You make me sick!

(She lowers the gun and hangs it back on the rack. JOCK takes a drink and starts laughing.)

JOCK: If it'd been me, sweetheart, I'da pulled the trigger. I'da blown you away like a bunny rabbit. . . *(He rocks back and forth with laughter. Silence.* SONIA *lies down on the bed.)*

The trouble with you, babe, you're too excitable. You're not a bad girl, just excitable.

(He drinks a while in silence. He goes over to the window and looks out. The rain is beating again the windowpane.) Fuck this goddamn shit! Look at it rain. *(A clap of thunder resounds.)* And thunder to boot. *(pause)* Hey, Sonia. You see this shit?

SONIA *(indifferent)*: No.

JOCK: It's raining fuckin' buckets. Flooding every goddamn where. It's like I'm livin' on some island somewhere. *(slight pause)* And when you think how I hate water. *(slight pause)* C'm 'ere and look at this, Sonia. Jesus, this is Niagara falls!. . . *(slight pause)* And thunder to boot. . . *(slight pause)* And when you think I can't even swim. *(slight pause)* Fuck this goddamn shit! Look at it rain! *(slight pause)* C'm 'ere and look at this! *(Slight pause)* I sure hope this window's sealed tight! *(slight pause)* And just think, this shit's falling outta the sky!

SONIA: What do you expect it to fall out of?

JOCK: Hey, me, I don't expect nothing. What do I care, let it rain! I'm just saying. *(slight pause)* It's beautiful. *(slight pause)* It's disgusting. . . *(slight pause)* But sure as hell beautiful. *(slight pause)* I remember one day I went to a movie with Kat, oh, a number of years ago, an' I remember it rained all through that film from beginning to end. . . *(slight pause)* It was a love story. . . *(slight pause)* Just another love story like all the rest. *(slight pause)* I remember, the tall guy kept kissing the girl in front of the window. . . *(slight pause)* An' outside the window, it was raining. *(slight pause)* The more he kissed her, the harder it rained. *(slight pause)* And when they made love in front of the window. . . *(slight pause)* there was a clap of thunder. *(slight pause)* That was the end of the movie, right at the thunder clap. Then lights came on in the theater. *(slight pause)* Everybody got up and left but us, me and Kat, we just sat there, kinda moved. Then the old ticket taker came down and said movie's over, we had to go, so we left. *(slight pause)* Outside it was snowing. *(slight pause)* I remember that very well. *(He continues to stare out the window, as if lost in a revery. SONIA is still lying on the bed, her glass in hand. Suddenly—)*

Jimmy! Jimmy! What the fuck are you doing in that kitchen!

SONIA: Oh shut up. Jimmy's gone out.

JOCK: Gone out? Where's he gone? *(She stares at him in silence.)* Where's my family, Lady?

SONIA *(annoyed)*: I swear you need to see a doctor! I don't know what kind of virus is eating you up inside, but it's wreaking havoc. If I were you, I'd get a major overhaul, if it's still possible!

JOCK *(coldly)*: Sonia. Where's Jimmy?

SONIA: I believe he still had some business to take care of at the meeting.

(She goes into the kitchen for a moment, then comes back.)

JOCK: Sweetheart, I've got something serious to say to you.

(She looks at him.) You hear me?!

SONIA: Bellowing like you do, I'd have to be deaf.

JOCK *(after a second)*: You know something, Lady? It really hurts me, it really pains me to see Jimmy foolin' around with that faggot. Mind you, I got nothing against queers, you know me, right? I'm broad-minded.

(She gives a reproving smile.)

Hell, we all sweat blood for what we think's good, but I . . . I just don't like that goddamn faggot Norman. He acts like he's some big-shot plantation owner or somethin'. When I was a kid I swore I'd kick his teeth down his throat, and now. . . there's just one more reason to do it.

SONIA: And what reason is that?

JOCK *(Drinks. Brief pause.)*: His gold teeth. *(He laughs.)*

SONIA: You poor dumb bastard! *(Slight pause. He keeps laughing.)*

JOCK: You know him? Tell me, sweetheart, you know Norman?

SONIA *(turning her back)*: Vaguely.

JOCK *(walking right behind her)*: Uh uh, Lady. You don't know Norman "vaguely." Either you love him or you hate him, one way or the other, simple as that.

SONIA: Okay, put it this way: he bought me a drink once and was very nice.

JOCK *(astonished)*: Nice?! ! That crab face? You say the guy bought you a drink?

SONIA: That right.

JOCK: He musta been drunk outta his mind.

SONIA: No, he was having coffee.

JOCK: Coffee!? *(He bursts out laughing.)* Where'd you guys get drunk?

SONIA: You're so boring.

JOCK: You wanta know something? *(He looks at her. After a moment.)*: You're beautiful, Sonia. Today, you're absolutely radiant, a heavenly star. . .

(She looks at him. He seems to soften.)

I'm in the presence of a star.

SONIA: Come off this!

JOCK: Soon enough you'll be even more beautiful, once I've lanced that canker inside.

(He chuckles and turns back to the window, glass in hand.)

SONIA *(after a while)*: Are you hungry?

JOCK: What for?

SONIA: What for? I'm asking if you're hungry! I'm asking do you want to eat! Why do we eat? In your opinion.

JOCK *(with a suspicious look)*: I have a very strong feeling that you've got something in mind, Lady.

SONIA: Huh? What do you mean something in mind?

JOCK: You know perfectly well what I'm talking about.

SONIA: Sorry, I don't get it.

JOCK: I see through your little game. You're trying to lure me on.

(SONIA bursts out laughing.)

SONIA: Lure you on? Lure you where?

(JOCK smiles.)

Lure you where, you dumb son-of-bitch!

(JOCK keeps smiling.)

JOCK: Don't play the innocent with me. You wanna wrap me aroun' your little finger, doncha? Well you're wasting your time, your little finger won't hold. And I don't like your legs anymore!

SONIA *(amused)*: How can you say that, when you can't even see them? My dress is too long.

JOCK *(Looking at her. Brief pause.)*: I don't like your dress for that matter. Leaves me cold.

(Takes a drink. After a moment.)

SONIA *(She takes a drink, then lifts her dress slightly, showing a little leg)*: How about this?

(JOCK stares in silence.)

You like my dress like this?

(JOCK stares at SONIA's legs, as if hypnotized.)

And wouldn't you like it like this? Like in the old days, Jock? When you used to chase me? Remember? And when you'd catch me and I refused? Huh? What do you say, Jock?

JOCK *(still staring at SONIA's legs as if in a daze)*: I say. . . I say shit!

(SONIA covers her legs. JOCK drinks. After a moment.)

SONIA: Work up an appetite now, Jock?

JOCK *(Disenchanted, he gives her a violent look.)*: No!

(Then more softly, as if he wished to please.)

My stomach feels like it's on fire.

SONIA: Well then maybe you should take up apple juice.

(Disgusted, he gives her a murderous look. After a while, SONIA starts laughing, as if she'd just remembered something. She sits down in the rocking chair.)

JOCK *(annoyed)*: What's so funny?

SONIA: Oh, nothing, I was just remembering a few little details concerning you.

JOCK: Oh? Like what?

SONIA: Like about before.

JOCK: Before what?

SONIA *(smiling with her head back, as if remembering)*: You used to spend all your time keeping an eye on Jimmy's comings and goings. *(She laughs.)*

JOCK: What is this crap?

SONIA *(laughing)*: As soon as he'd get his coat on to go out, you'd start champing at the bit, and once the car started, the stampede would start all over again!

JOCK: What stampede?

SONIA: You remember when you locked us in the shed? *(She laughs.)* Right after you did it you had to break the door down, didn't you? Remember?

(JOCK looks at her violently.)

You got scared that day, didn't you? You were afraid Jimmy might come back too soon.

JOCK: Liar! *(He takes a swig.)*

SONIA: I didn't like the way you ran after me back then, I was afraid of you. I used to tremble at the very smell of you behind me, I couldn't stand the way you used to.

JOCK *(cutting her off)*: You little piece of shit!

SONIA *(calmly)*: Now don't get all excited, Jock. And don't get on your high horse. It's not my fault you fell down those stairs running after me.

(He smiles.)

You should've watched where you were going. Nobody made you take me into that barn, and nobody made you chop off your leg on that scythe, trying to rape me.

JOCK: Rape you! But that's exactly what you wanted!

SONIA *(laughing)*: Thing is, you see, that day, someone was watching over us from above, someone who made up his mind that snakes like you deserve to end up as cripples.

(JOCK stares at her violently. Silence. She stares up at the ceiling. Then, calmly:)

Would you like something to eat now?

JOCK *(coldly, after a moment)*: You know what would really please me, sweetheart?

SONIA: No. What would really please you?

JOCK: I'd like to be able to draw.

SONIA: No kidding!

JOCK: Yeah. 'Cause if I could really draw well, I'd draw me a tree, an African tree way out in the middle of nowhere. Then I'd draw hundreds of gorillas, big fat gorillas without their females, all around the tree, and then, I'd draw you, strapped to the tree, completely naked, and you'd be the only woman in the picture, and up in the sky above your head, buzzards would be circling around and around. It would all be so peaceful, except of course right around the tree, and then, I'd draw a sunset, a beautiful African sunset, and the picture would be finished. Then I'd hang it on the wall and I swear to you I'd stop every time I passed it, I'd get a real bang out of that, and you—you'd be finished, completely finished.

SONIA: At times you know, you're a real poet, even if you do have one basic problem, you're a real poet.

(JOCK casts a sidelong glance at her and takes a drink before replying.)

JOCK: What basic problem?

SONIA: Oh come on, Jock, don't be an idiot, you know very well what I'm talking about.

(They look at each other.)

Too bad, too bad for you.

(She gets up, goes to the bar to pour herself a drink. After a while, still at the bar, she turns around and lifts up her dress a little. JOCK stares at her legs, fascinated.)

JOCK *(visibly affected)*: What are you doing?

(Silence. He stares.)

What are you doing, Sonia? *(slight pause)*: Lower that, willya? *(slight pause)* Sonia! Lower that dress!

(She looks at him. Slight pause.)

SONIA *(calmly, almost girlishly)*: Why? Why should I lower it? *(slight pause)* After all, you still have your hands, don't you? *(slight pause)* She smiles and lifts her dress a little higher. He still stares.

JOCK: Lower it, Sonia lower it, it's too repulsive!

SONIA *(smiling)*: Isn't that right, Mr. Gladiator? You still have your hands.

JOCK *(very aroused)*: Oh yes, oh yes, I still have my hands, and. . . and other things too.

SONIA *(feigning astonishment and interest)*: Oooh, really? I had no idea.

JOCK *(standing up)*: Sonia! Don't play around like this, please!

(He approaches her, she moves back as if playing a game.)

My little Sonia I. . .

SONIA *(still backing away quietly)*: What's that? What's that you say?

(She smiles. JOCK walks painfully toward her.)

JOCK: I. . . I. . .

SONIA *(dress still lifted)*: You what? Say it, Jock tell it to me, please, my dear, tell me that you want it.

(Both still moving, he seems more and more aroused.)

JOCK: Yes.

SONIA: You're trying to say that you want it!

JOCK: Yes, yes, I want it, I want it very much.

SONIA: More than that!

JOCK: Huh?

SONIA: You want it much more than that!

JOCK: Yes yes, that's right, that's right, that's true.

SONIA: What's right, Jock? What's true?

JOCK: That. . . that I really do want it, I want it enormously, that I. . . want it much more than that!

SONIA: Oh? and how long has it been?

JOCK: Since forever!

SONIA: That's not what I asked!

JOCK: Huh?

SONIA: You stupid cretin. I asked you how long has it been.

JOCK: How long has it been. . . since what?

SONIA: Since you put your hands on a woman!

(The rhythm of the dialogue returns to normal.)

JOCK *(very agitated)*: I. . . I. . . Sonia!

(He falls down. She stops backing away.)

Sonia my love, I. . . I beg of you.

(He touches her feet and calves with the tips of his fingers.)

My darling. . .

(She kicks him.)

No, no, don't do that.

(Very brief silence as they look at one another.)

Darling, my darling, I love you, you're my whole life,
I want. . .

*(He manages to touch her legs. He seems completely
subjugated.)*

SONIA *(contemptuously)*: What I like about you is that
you're a real chameleon. This ability of yours to
change from bulldog to cockroach is truly amazing.
Sometimes you're up on your high horse, next thing
you're crawling around on the floor playing doormat.

JOCK *(as if hypnotised by her legs)*: I want to touch. . .
I. . . touch you.

SONIA *(She moves away again)*: Tell me, Jock! You
know that house over on the lake?

JOCK *(He keeps trying more or less successfully to touch
her legs)*: What house?

SONIA: You know perfectly well what house, we've
already discussed it.

JOCK *(still at it)*: Oh yeah! You want I guess to talk
about the. . . the tower?

SONIA: Exactly. About the tower.

*(They stare at each other for a few seconds, she still
standing, he still on the floor.)*

JOCK: You came back here to. . . to put me away in
that place, didn't you?

(They look at each other. SONIA smiles strangely.)

Okay! Let's suppose. Suppose that. . . I'd like to go away to that place.

SONIA *(with a big smile)*: Just for a little while, my joy, nothing more than that, just one quick little visit and no more, purely routine, they won't hurt you, they'll just write a few prescriptions and you'll be on your way, that's all, no big deal.

JOCK *(staring at her avidly)*: Just one. . . teeny little visit. and that's it.

SONIA: That's it, exactly.

JOCK: Does that. . . could that maybe mean that. . . that I can touch you?

SONIA *(with a smile)*: Of course, Jock! obviously that's what that could mean.

(She runs her hands over her legs. He watches, bug-eyed.)

JOCK *(after a moment)*: I. . . I gotta think. *(He stares at her legs.)* This isn't an easy decision to make.

(She lifts her dress a little higher.)

Okay! I agree to the little visit. *(He quietly comes closer.)* Anything you want.

(He arrives at her knees. They stare at one another. After a brief moment, he starts caressing her legs. She says nothing, remains motionless. Then higher and higher up, he stares at SONIA's legs, then his hands disappear beneath her dress; they stare at

each other again, JOCK *with his mouth open, as if in ecstasy. After a moment—)*

SONIA: Not so hard. *(Pause. Obviously he hasn't heard. She grabs a handful of his hair.)* I said not so hard!

JOCK: Yes! Yes. Not so hard. . . *(He seems in a daze of pleasure.)* Right. Not so hard.

(She grimaces more and more, as he rubs his face against her legs, licks them, and seems on the point of orgasm. At which point she shoves him away, he falls down in the middle of the room. SONIA *goes to pour a drink, while* JOCK *lies there, still in a daze. She watches him slowly recover, drinking.)*

SONIA *(After a while. Needling him)*: So. . . did we get off on that?

(She smiles sullenly. JOCK *shakes his head and tries to get up, not knowing what to say—still under the influence of his emotion.)*

Now. There are some promises that are going to have to be kept, my sweet. . . *(Takes a sip. He tries again to get up.)*

A promise is a promise.

(He manages to stand up and goes to the bar for a drink.)

I'm talking to you!

JOCK *(almost as if just waking up)*: Huh? Oh yeah.

SONIA: You sure you understood what I just said?

85

JOCK: Yeah. *(He takes a drink, apparently thinking. To SONIA.)* No.

SONIA: No!? No what?

JOCK: I didn't get what you said.

SONIA *(not answering immediately, she takes a drink)*: I asked you not to forget about your promise.

JOCK: What promise? Oh yeah, of course! My promise. . . *(He drinks.)* I completely forgot. *(He starts snickering.)*

SONIA: Otherwise, there'll be no more caresses, Jock, never again.

JOCK *(still laughing)*: Look, Sonia if I go into that big house, there won't be any more caresses anyway, am I right? 'Cause they won't ever let me out of there. *(He smiles.)*

SONIA: Don't be silly. I really don't believe that's true. And anyway, I can always come see you.

JOCK: Come see me? Wow!. . .Now there's an idea. I never even thought of that.

SONIA: Of course! it's a great idea! And we'd never tell a soul. . . it'd be like our own little secret, wouldn't it? Just between you and me.

JOCK: That's really a great idea.

SONIA: And then we'll play our domino games, too, Jock, just like we used to when you won all the time. . . *(slight pause)* You'll never be short another six, or another two, or anything, Jock. In fact, you'll never lack anything ever again.

JOCK *(with a sidelong glance)*: You mean. . . the same kind of domino games?

SONIA: I mean exactly the same.

JOCK: Only this time, you can't run away.

SONIA: Well of course not.

JOCK *(apparently thinking)*: Or put it this way: You'll try to run away, only this time not so fast.

SONIA: Of course! Whatever you want.

JOCK *(looking at her, after a moment)*: Okay, I'm game!

SONIA *(clearly pleased)*: Really and truly?

JOCK: Really and truly, Lady!

SONIA *(goes over to him laughing)*: I think I'd like to have this dance, darling!

(Without giving him the chance to reply, she seizes him and starts to dance. He seems to be losing his balance.)

JOCK *(ill-at-ease)*: I don't know how to dance! I don't know how to dance, Lady.

(She releases him and goes to get her glass as well as JOCK's. *She hands it to him.)*

You win!

(They drink.)

Anyway, I couldn't sleep anymore on that pallet, you know, Lady? Can't bear the sight of it anymore. *(He takes a drink.)* Now this is gonna change my whole life. . .

(They both smile.)

And yet, there's just one thing that bugs me.

SONIA *(afraid he's changing his mind)*: What's that?

JOCK *(looking out the window)*: The rain is slacking up.

I don't like the lake. You think they'll put me in a room with a view on the lake?

SONIA: Of course not! All you have to do is ask for one on the other side.

JOCK: What other side, my sweet?

SONIA: On the side facing the land!

JOCK: Oh! They have a view over the land too?

SONIA: But of course, Jock of course they do.

JOCK: Well in that case everything's for the best! And now that I think of it, all those little nurses will be comin' around within an arm's reach. I gotta think it's worth a visit, don't you, Lady?

SONIA: For sure, you're in for a real treat.

JOCK: I know I can make it with some of those little tarts, don't you? What do you think?

SONIA: No problem.

JOCK: The hardest part is getting 'em to the door of the toilet, but you gotta do it, no way around it, and then, you can't let 'em get a word in edgewise—after that, it's all in the bag.

SONIA: For sure, Jock for sure!

JOCK *(seeming to search his memory)*: Damn thing is, what do I use for an excuse? I don't have the imagination I used to when I was twenty. . .to find the right excuse. *(He takes a drink.)*

SONIA: You have one, Jock.

JOCK: Really?

SONIA: Your leg! You've got your leg!

JOCK *(He stares at her a few seconds)*: Yeahhh.you're right, sweetheart, I've got my leg. . . or maybe we should say. . . *(Slight pause as he looks at his leg.)* You're right—it's the perfect excuse.

(They drink.)

SONIA: Tell me!

JOCK: Mmm?

SONIA: I was thinking about something.

(He looks her way.)

I. . . uh. . . I don't want to bother you with this, but. . . I really think it might be a better idea if we left before Jimmy comes back.

JOCK: Huh?. . . Oh yes! Quite right, sweetheart, I know he's not gonna be exactly thrilled at the idea.

(She casts him a sidelong glance. He takes a drink.)

Well, then good, let's get ready.

(He puts his glass down.)

Hey, sweetheart! Just one little question.

SONIA: I'm listening.

JOCK: How we gonna make our way down there?

SONIA: We're gonna borrow Miss Dideaux's buggy.

JOCK: Why not just take the bus?

(SONIA begins to take some of JOCK's clothes out of the closet.)

SONIA: There is no more bus.

JOCK *(finishing his glass)*: And since when is there no more bus?

SONIA: Listen, what difference does it make how we get there? All I can tell you is, we'll make it, I can promise you that.

(JOCK sits motionless, watching SONIA busy herself.)

JOCK: Since when is there no more bus, Lady?

SONIA *(sighing)*: Since there was no more gas.

JOCK: Oh! *(He pours himself another drink.)* So, let me get this straight: we're gonna make this trip on some goddamn horses or somethin'. *(Takes a swig.)* I don't like horses.

SONIA: Listen. You and I, we'll be in the wagon. These godamn horses, as you call them, they will be up front, we're not going to ride them.

JOCK *(drinking)*: Whatever. I don't like to ride horses. *(He takes his glass over to the window.)* It's almost stopped raining.

(He takes a drink, while SONIA packs his bags.)

And if it starts up again out there, what do we do then?

SONIA: We'll find shelter.

JOCK *(still staring out the windowpane)*: Very clever. Where?

SONIA: We'll see when the time comes. In the meantime, get dressed!

JOCK *(He turns to face her, surprised)*: But Lady, I am dressed!

SONIA: So put on your overcoat.

JOCK: Oh yeah, my overcoat.

(He starts to go put on his overcoat. Then he stops for a moment, in the attitude of one who has just remembered something.)

Lady?

SONIA: What!

JOCK *(after a moment's reflection)*: Before anything, I have to tell you something very important.

SONIA: I'm listening.

JOCK: Yeah. I just thought of this.

SONIA *(Looks at him. Slight pause.)*: Thought of what?

JOCK *(slight pause)*: I just think that. . . I think I would like for you and the buggy and the rain and Miss Dideaux to all go get yourselves royally fucked!

SONIA *(trying not to lose her composure)*: Do you now? And why would that be?

JOCK: Because. . . because I had forgotten all about one important detail.

SONIA: No kidding! And what is this detail?

JOCK: My seashells, Lady.

SONIA (*trying not to explode*): What do you mean?

JOCK: I mean that you didn't consider my shells, did you. I can't abandon them just like that! Don't forget: these are the most beautiful specimens you're ever gonna find! If I left them behind for this tower, Lady, I could never sleep in peace again.

SONIA (*beside herself*): You've never slept with your seashells, as far as I know! Just bring them with you!

JOCK: What? Uh uh, Lady, not possible. I have nine thousand three hundred and twenty-five of them—no, nine thousand three hundred and twenty-six now, Jimmy's being the most beautiful of all. No, I can't, it's impossible, I can't take them out of their natural habitat. It'd kill them!

SONIA: Don't talk nonsense, Jock. The natural habitat of a seashell is the beach, not a cellar!

JOCK: This is no ordinary cellar. We have sand, and there's even some sea water.

SONIA: I thought you didn't like water.

JOCK (*dressed to go out*): It's the lake I don't like, Sonia. Not the same. Sea water, I've got nothing against.

(*Brief moment of silence. JOCK sits down in his rocking chair.*)

If I take them, I'll kill them.

SONIA: No. I'll kill you!

JOCK: Now, there, sweetheart, don't get mad—try to
understand. One's environment is so important. This
is the ideal cellar. If you could only see them,
they're so *brilliant*. . . It'd be a crime to take them
out of there.

SONIA: Give me the keys, I think I can handle it.

JOCK: No! I'm sorry, Lady, nobody touches those keys!
Nobody has gone down into that cellar except me,
you understand? That's my place! It is absolutely
forbidden to set foot in my cellar! I made an
agreement with Jimmy, and that's good enough for
you! No, Lady, sorry, there's nothing I can do.

(SONIA *seems to relax.* JOCK *is still in his rocking
chair.*)

Anyway, you'd never know how to talk to them.
(slight pause) I do, I know how to talk to them.
(slight pause) The tone of voice is so important.
(slight pause) The volume, too, that's important.
(Slight pause. Louder.) You must never shout!
(Slight pause. Very softly.) Otherwise, they die.
(slight pause) Then the content! Hah! the content!
You can't just go in there and say any ol' thing.
(slight pause) If you don't take every precaution,
they can just fade away. *(He drinks.)* That's why it's
not possible, Lady.

SONIA *(relaxed, almost smiling)*: Oh, well, it's no big deal, I just. . . I was just thinking aloud, I thought maybe for you it might've been a good idea to get some rest for a while, that's all.

JOCK *(feigning emotion)*: Thank you, my dear, thank you for thinking of my health.

SONIA: Think nothing of it. *(slight pause)*: Can I get you a drink?

JOCK *(almost surprised)*: Sure, by all means.

(She pours him a drink.)

You don't hold it against me, do you?

SONIA *(bringing his glass)*: No! Not at all, don't worry about it.

(She's wearing a smile, and seems slightly drunk.)

JOCK *(smiling in turn)*: So now, you can just put my things back in the closet.

SONIA: Oh yes, of course, I'll do it afterwards *(She takes a drink)*

JOCK: I'm happy you're taking it like this, and you know, just between you and me, I never would've done very well in that place, don't you think?

SONIA: That's quite possible, Jock, quite possible.

JOCK: And as a matter of fact, I'm beginning to understand what's behind all this.

SONIA: Oh, really?

JOCK: That's right.

SONIA: Well let's hear.

JOCK: Well, the bottom line is, you had a problem.

SONIA: Meaning?

JOCK *(taking a drink)*: All you needed was just a little more privacy with Jimmy, right Sonia? So it occurs to you this idea of the tower on the lake might not be a bad solution. But you know, Sonia I realize you didn't hatch this little plot just 'cause you don't like me, you just wanted to be alone with Jimmy, am I wrong there, sweetheart?

SONIA: No, Jock you're not wrong. *(She takes a drink.)* On the contrary, I like you, but. . . but you're right in saying that. . . that, for our privacy, Jimmy's and mine, obviously. . .

JOCK: . . .it wasn't ideal.

SONIA: Yes.

JOCK: Yeah, I understand, I understand, sweetheart. From now on, I'm gonna try to make like a little easier on you two and just keep out of the way.

(SONIA stares at him. He drinks. Brief moment.)

That way, you guys can screw to your heart's content in complete privacy, somewhere else! *(He snickers.)* You see, sweetheart, I am going to make an effort.

(SONIA *takes a sip.*)

SONIA *(with a murderous look)*: I'm overwhelmed by your sense of sacrifice.

(It starts raining again furiously. The sound of thunder.)

JOCK: Think nothing of it, it's only natural. *(He takes a drink.)* To begin with, we'll trade beds. I wanna to get my mattress back, I'm tired of sleeping on that goddamn pallet, scratchin' away like some dog by the door. *(Takes a drink.)* It's different for you guys, you're young. At your age, I could sleep on a dungheap with no problem.

SONIA: Doesn't surprise me in the least.

(JOCK drinks, then starts rocking in his chair. SONIA, completely immobile, stares at him, her glass in hand. The floors creaks under the rocking chair. Outside, the rain increases in force. The room is badly lit. From time to time a flash of lightning from outside pierces the dark. After a while, JOCK gets up, goes to the window and looks out.)

JOCK *(nostalgic)*: Fuck this goddamn weather, look at it pour!

(A clap of thunder. Slight pause.)

Makes you wonder where it's gonna end.

(Slight pause. Still without looking at her.)

Come look at this, sweetheart! One thing's for sure, this is fuckin' Niagara Falls! *(slight pause)* Come look at this, love!

(She takes a drink, then goes to join him at the window. Slight pause.)

Can you believe it!?

(He slips his arm around her waist. She says nothing.)

It's beautiful!

(They both look out, as if awed by the rain. Slight pause.)

It's disgusting, but it's beautiful. *(slight pause)* I'm going to leave you now, sweetheart, got to go pay my little friends a visit, chat with 'em a little. . .

(He caresses her hair then moves toward the cellar door. He fumbles for the key in his pockets, finds it, opens the two locks, then suddenly stops. . .

For several seconds, each in his corner, they stand transfixed, like wax statues. Nevertheless, the rain is still audible and several flashes of lightning are seen. Then JOCK turns around, and. . .)

Say, sweetheart, can I tell 'em hello for you?

(SONIA doesn't answer. He goes down into the cellar laughing, closes the door behind him without locking it. SONIA stays by the window for several seconds. Outside the rain doubles in intensity.

She goes to the bar, pours a drink, and gulps it down. For several seconds she remains immobile; she seems drained, livid. She goes over to the cellar door, tries to open it, and the door swings open. For once, JOCK has forgotten to lock it behind him. She closes it, goes back to the bar, and has another drink. Her features have hardened, her face betrays a certain determination. She drinks in quick little gulps.

She puts down her glass and goes over to the shotgun. She takes it down, checks to see if there are cartridges in the barrel, then closes it. She goes to the door of the cellar, opens it, and starts to go down the stairs.

After a few moments, during which there are several flashes of lightning and claps of thunder, the sound of two shotgun blasts is heard coming from the cellar, followed by the sound of body falling, then another noise which could be sea-shells.

For several seconds nothing more is heard. Then again, another sound, that of a body being dragged, then the clatter of wood and iron being hammered together.

After a while, she comes back up. She seems exhausted, her hair is in total disarray, her dress is stained with black. She hangs the gun back up on the wall, then pours another drink which she downs in one gulp.

After a while she seems to regain her spirits. She grabs JOCK's bag off a chair, as well as several other personal effects such as his cane.

She goes back down to the cellar with all of this. We hear the same clatter of wood and iron, then she comes back up, examines the room to make sure that none of JOCK's *possessions are left lying around.*

She closes the cellar door and locks the double lock, and for several seconds, stands there immobile, in the attitude of one trying to figure out what to do next.

She looks down at the keys. She picks up her overcoat, puts it on, then a slicker over that. She puts the keys in her pocket then starts to go out.

She opens the front door, then closes it. After a moment's hesitation, she goes back to the shotgun, takes it down, opens it, and removes the two empty cartridges. She puts these in her pocket as well. She goes over to the wardrobe, opens it, and takes two new cartridges out of a box which she inserts in the shotgun before replacing it on the wall.

She moves again toward the front door, turns around and casts one last glance over the room, then exits.

Curtain.)